W9-BVE-864

# A CHURCH GUIDE FOR STRENGTHENING FAMILIES

# A CHURCH GUIDE FOR STRENGTHENING FAMILIES

## STRATEGIES, MODELS, PROGRAMS, AND RESOURCES

### JIM LARSON

**AUGSBURG** Publishing House • Minneapolis

**A CHURCH GUIDE FOR STRENGTHENING FAMILIES**
**Strategies, Models, Programs, and Resources**

This book was originally commissioned by the Strengthening Families Task Force of the National Council of Churches' Commission on Family Ministries and Human Suffering.

Scripture quotations unless otherwise noted are from the Revised Standard Version of the Bible, copyright 1946, 1952, and 1971 by the Division of Christian Education of the National Council of Churches.

**Library of Congress Cataloging-in-Publication Data**

Larson, Jim, 1942–
    A CHURCH GUIDE FOR STRENGTHENING FAMILIES.

    Bibliography: p.
    1. Family—Religious life.   I. Title.
BV4526.2.L3     1986        253        86-7965
ISBN 0-8066-2217-2

Manufactured in the U.S.A.                                    APH 10-1320

1    2    3    4    5    6    7    8    9    0    1    2    3    4    5    6    7    8    9

# Contents

Preface                                                        7
Acknowledgments                                                9
Introduction                                                  11

**Part One: Foundations**
Introduction                                                  13
Foundations in Faith                                          14
Historical Development                                        16
Current Trends                                                18
Family Wellness: A Focus for Ministry                         25
A Time for Advocacy                                           30

**Part Two: Implementation**
Introduction                                                  32
Strategizing for Family Ministry: An Overview                 32
Leadership Development                                        39

**Part Three: Models for Enhancing Family Wellness**
Introduction                                                  47
A Model for Marriage Enrichment                               48
A Model for Parent Education                                  55
A Model for Family Enrichment                                 61

**Part Four: Additional Resources**
Foundations                                                   72
Implementation                                                75
Marriage Enrichment                                           77
Resources for Couples                                         78
Parent Education                                              83
Resources for Parents                                         84
Family Enrichment                                             89
Resources for Families                                        90

Family Counseling 91
Training Organizations 93

## Part Five: Reproduction Masters

RM  1  Family Life Cycle 96
RM  2  Family Ministry through the Life Cycle 97
RM  3  Evaluation Tool for Developing Family Awareness 98
RM  4  Qualities of a Healthy Marriage and Family 99
RM  5  Bridge Building Exercise 100
RM  6  Marriage Time Line 101
RM  7  Marriage Inventory 102
RM  8  Resources for Couples 103
RM  9  When I Stop to Think about It . . . . 105
RM 10  Styles of Parenting 106
RM 11  Evaluating My Own Style of Parenting 107
RM 12  Personally Speaking 108
RM 13  Joys and Frustrations of Family Life 109
RM 14  Resources for Parents 110
RM 15  Wacky Words 1 112
RM 16  Family Fun Songs 113
RM 17  What the World Needs Now . . . . 114
RM 18  Wacky Words 2 115
RM 19  Family Togetherness 116
RM 20  Family Contract 117
RM 21  Wacky Words 3 118
RM 22  Patterns of Communication 119
RM 23  Family Situations 120
RM 24  Christian Songs for Families 121
RM 25  Brain Teasers 123
RM 26  Writing a Cinquain Poem 125
RM 27  Resources for Families 126

Notes 127

# PREFACE

The Commission on Family Ministries and Human Sexuality has been organized to develop cooperative study, research, experimentation, policy, resources and programs to assist churches in:

- The educational task of the home;
- The fulfillment of their responsibility for strengthening marriage and familial living through advocacy of adequate laws and sound policies and through programs of education, counseling, guidance, training, and leadership development;
- The concerns with human sexuality throughout the life cycle;
- The support of persons who find themselves in transition with regards to changing sex roles and family patterns.

Membership on the commission includes a wide spectrum of church denominations and other groups. Representatives on the commission generally are responsible for the area of family ministries in their respective groups.

In addition to the concerns and issues which are a primary focus at each commission meeting, the group is divided into several task forces, such as Strengthening Families, Violence and Families, and Justice and Families.

It has been the intent of the Task Force on Strengthening Families to develop these resources for your use. Whether you are professionally involved in family ministries or are seeking to implement such ministries as a layperson in the local church, these materials will provide you with a basic orientation and plan for family ministries.

Our hope and prayer is that these resources may give you a stronger motivation and a specific plan for nurturing healthy families.

ARTHUR O. VAN ECK, ED. D.
Executive Director
Education for Christian Life
and Mission

# ACKNOWLEDGMENTS

There are a number of persons who have made a significant contribution to this project:

- The members of the Commission on Family Ministries and Human Sexuality, who have encouraged and supported the development of these resources.
- The members of the Task Force on Strengthening Families— who have brainstormed, interacted, and evaluated the materials at every stage of the process. John Vogelsang, Ruth Mac-Donald, Margaret Sawin, Mary Matz, Mary Clare, Del Vander Haar, Ron Brusius, and Betty Brusius have shared their insights and expertise in special ways.
- The groups of couples, parents, and families with whom many of these resources were originally experienced.
- My own family members, who have provided such a nurturing framework in which to experience family love and health.

JIM LARSON

# INTRODUCTION

The concepts of "family" and of "family ministries" are both at interesting crossroads today.

There has been much debate recently about what a family actually is, and what its role should be. There have been significant transitions and changes which have affected family life in every aspect.

There has also been a growing interest in family ministries within local churches and denominations. But frequently there has been a hesitation or unsureness about what steps to take—where to begin, what to do, and with whom to do it.

The purpose of this book is to provide both professional and lay leaders in the local church with resources which are intended to:

- Describe and evaluate trends and transitions affecting family life.
- Identify a basic framework and goals for family ministry.
- Give guidelines for implementing family ministry and developing the needed leadership.
- Outline a specific plan for enriching marriage and family relationships.
- List resources for additional reading and implementation.

Notice that the last section of this book contains a series of Re-production Masters, (to be abbreviated as RM in the following pages) which you can photocopy and use in a variety of workshops and learning experiences.

May God deepen your insights and bless your efforts at facilitating the growth of healthy families.

# PART ONE

# FOUNDATIONS

## Introduction

For centuries, people have expressed decidedly mixed feelings about the institution we call the family.

For example, researcher Albert J. Solnit maintains:

> Even if we all decided that the family unit had outlived its usefulness and that we could create a better setting for children and adults based on our best knowledge of human development, it is predictable that we would rediscover the dynamic human arrangement we call the family. The family is a nourishing, protective, guiding group that also provides a meaningful bridge from the past to the future.[1]

Indeed, there have been many advocates of the family over the years. But there have also been those who wonder why families are needed. Author Gail Godwin raises this question in her recent novel *A Mother and Two Daughters:*

> What made them imprison themselves in the separate pressure cookers referred to as "nuclear families"? Of course, children didn't form them; children came to consciousness and found themselves already bubbling away in the pot. But then what made these children grow up and start another pressure cooker of their own? . . . First the smug exclusion of all others, of the "outside world"; then the grim multiplication of oneself and one's partner behind closed doors; then the nauseating, unclean moiling about of all the family members in their "nuclear" cauldron, bumping against one another, everyone knowing all too well everyone else's worst faults—all of them *stewing* themselves in one another's juices.[2]

During the past few decades, there has been increasing discussion regarding whether or not families had become merely an outmoded tradition of the past, or if they are undergoing some rather major transitions and changes while yet being vital for healthy human development.

In this chapter, we will explore foundational concerns related to the question of the importance and purpose of families. In addition to an overview of what the Christian community has believed regarding families, we will review some of the more important trends as they have had influence on what family units have experienced.

We will also explore the idea of family wellness as a focus for family ministry.

## Foundations in Faith

From the very beginning of biblical history, families were seen as vital. After God had created the world, the Scriptures tell us that one person (Adam) was created. Then God said, "It is not good that man should be alone" (Gen. 2:18); so Eve was created. Thus, from the earliest days, relationships have been acknowledged as the context for healthy growth and development. And intimacy is described as an essential component of our relationships (Gen. 2:24).

In the early chapters of biblical history, family relationships emerge repeatedly as a primary focus. For example, the stories of Cain and Abel, Abraham and Sarah, Jacob and Esau, and Joseph and his brothers deal with the kinds of problems and concerns which are still relevant to families today: jealousy, one-upmanship, favoritism, love, and commitment.

In a time when there was great immigration, migration, famines, and flood, God used family units as a means of *historical continuity.* The legacies of one generation were passed down from one generation to the next (Deut. 4:9-10).

But God had more in mind for families, which were valued as a means of *spiritual continuity* as well—the passing on of the legacy of faith from one generation to another.

The home was perceived as the place where the most vital learning would take place, whether formally or informally:

> Teach them to your children. Repeat them when you are at home and when you are away, when you are resting and when you are working. Tie them on your arms and wear them on your foreheads as a reminder. Write them on the doorposts of your houses and on your gates (Deut. 6:7-9 TEV).

Throughout the Scriptures, the role of parent was seen as vital, even awesome. Parenting was seen as an experience which could produce both joy and grief (see Prov. 10:1; 17:25; 23:24).

Rebellion of children and youth against their parents has been apparent since biblical times. Repeatedly, the Scriptures exhorted children to listen to their parents (see Prov. 1:8; 4:1-2,4), and also exhorted parents to do right by their children (see Eph. 6).

And parenting was perceived as a joint responsibility, not merely the primary domain of either mother or father (see Prov. 1:8; 6:20).

The New Testament Scriptures continued these same assumptions regarding the importance of families. During his earthly ministry, Jesus seemed to enjoy children. He was an intergenerational teacher who rebuked the disciples when they tried to keep the children from him (see Matt. 19:13-15). Jesus maintained that children are examples of faith and trust who are worthy of emulation by adults.

We find repeated references in the New Testament to the vital importance of the care of children in families (see Matt. 7:11). Parents were expected to be sensitive to the needs of their children and to guide them to become healthy, mature adults (see 2 Cor. 12:14; Eph. 6:4).

The family relationship was one which people could understand. So, as Jesus taught many important truths regarding God, faith and life, he often used the analogy of the parent-child relationship to refer to how God related to the people of faith (see Matt. 5:45, 48; 7:7-11).

Repeatedly in the Scriptures, people are challenged to grow individually in qualities which have a relational as well as a personal component. In this way, faith can deepen one's personal growth while it strengthens one's ability to live in relationships which are loving, supportive, and kind—the qualities that are exhibited in God's relationship with people (see Gal. 5:22-23, for example).

Since the times in which the Scriptures were written, families have been perceived as a primary context for healthy growth and development—physically, emotionally, socially, and spiritually. This growth is intended to take place for adults as well as children, for children can have great influence—either positively or negatively on their parents, just as parents can have great influence on the development of their children.

## Historical Development

One quickly recognizes that there have been major changes in how families function over the past two thousand years.

Going back three or four hundred years, we find that many families living in a rural setting were largely self-sufficient. Most of them grew enough crops and had enough animals to take care of themselves, for the most part. In such homes everyone, including young children, played important productive roles in planting and harvesting crops as well as maintenance of the family itself.

By the 19th century, all of this began to change. Farm families began to specialize by raising one crop for sale. The days of being self-sufficient were over for many of these families as the number of people living in towns and cities grew.

During those years, families were often responsible for the education of their children. Whatever reading and writing skills children possessed were usually taught at home, as were basic religious attitudes and values.

But, with the coming of the Industrial Revolution and the specialization of work that it brought, some major changes began to take place in the family. As life became more complex, the days when families could be entirely self-sufficient were definitely numbered.

At this point, we must acknowledge a difference of opinion among family researchers regarding these trends. Even though a great number of families did live on farms, and there was indeed a major shift for them to a more urban setting, there were also families who lived in cities all along. For them, these transitions may not have been as dramatic. They lived more interdependently than probably did most of their counterparts who had been farmers.

There is also the factor of race and other ethnic backgrounds for many families. What may have been true for families in one ethnic or racial group may have been somewhat different for others. While some families may have been largely self-sufficient, for example, other families may not have been.

Yet, no matter what our perspective on family development over the past 200 years, there have been several noticeable transitions which have affected many families:

- Since the development of public schools, formal education has generally replaced family education rather than assisted it. Today, for a total of at least 14–16 years, the typical child spends the better part of most weekdays away from home, and in the presence of nonrelated teachers and children.
- Families have a changing role in the care of the aged. Government has generally become a primary source of financial support for many elderly people, for example.
- The imparting of basic religious attitudes and values is now often perceived as the responsibility of the church and other religious organizations. Still, parents are sometimes unaware of the direct and indirect ways in which they model values which their children imitate, for better or for worse.
- Social development is often facilitated through children's involvement in day care, clubs, sports, and school organizations. Many children have become peer-oriented and less oriented towards being with their families.

The impact of these and other changes is that in many ways, there are reduced expectations for families. For example, mothers are not necessarily expected to be the primary caregiver for their preschool-age children. Fathers are not expected to train their children in skills for a job. And parents are not expected to teach academic skills, as they may have in previous centuries.

Other institutions with technical expertise have taken over many of these functions. Consequently, the parent often has more of a management role than a direct function with children. Much of the parent's time may be taken up with choosing schools, doctors, special programs, consulting with teachers, monitoring television watching, and so on, rather than in direct contact with children.

Thus, parents are often perceived as those who supplement and support that which takes place at school and church, rather than being perceived as the key persons in their children's developmental process.

Consequently, today's parents may feel they have little authority or power over those with whom they share the task of raising children. Parents may see themselves as dealing from a position of inferiority or helplessness, without a voice, authority, or power.

If many of these traditional functions have been removed from families, then what is the purpose of families today? Increasingly, the role of families is to fulfill the emotional needs of parents and children.

Researcher Kenneth Keniston states it this way:

> With work life highly impersonal, ties with neighbors tenuous, and truly intimate out-of-family friendships rare, husbands and wives tend to put all of their emotional hope for fulfillment into their family life. Expectations of sharing, sexual compatibility, and temperamental harmony in marriage have risen as other family functions have diminished.[3]

In other words, since work has become more technical and impersonal for many people, their needs for closeness may be transferred more and more to family relationships. While some functions of family life seemed to have changed, the need for intimacy and love still exists. And if persons expect their families to meet all of their emotional and relational needs, their families may feel stressed by these great expectations.

## Current Trends

There are a number of trends and patterns which are impacting family functioning, whether directly or more subtly. Such dynamics as technological change, economic realities, relational transitions, moral perplexities and church traditions need to be acknowledged and explored.

## Technological Change

There is no doubt that an avalanche of technological development has moved us quite abruptly into a new age.

Alvin Toffler provides us with a graphic example of how quickly change has taken place in our culture. He says that if we divide the last 50,000 years of human existence into lifetimes of approximately 62 years each, there would have been about 800 such lifetimes. Of these, fully 650 were spent in caves. Only during the past 70 lifetimes have people been able to communicate effectively through writing. During the past six lifetimes, we have seen the development of the printed word. And it has been only during the past two lifetimes that there has been an electric motor. Most material goods we use daily have been developed within the present, 800th lifetime!

Research indicates that approximately three-fourths of the data and information we have today was not available to us at the close of World War II. For children born in the 1970s, cumulative world knowledge will have quadrupled by the time they graduate from college. And by the time that these people have reached age 50, 97% of everything known in the world will have been learned since they were born.

In recent years, we have felt the growing impact of this growth in knowledge and technology on our families, given the advent of the home computer, video games, and the like.

And television continues to have its impact as well. Research indicates that by age 16, a typical child will have watched 12,000 to 15,000 hours of television. By the time children become adults, they will have spent more time watching television than attending school or being with their families.

It has been over fifteen years since Toffler introduced the concept of "future shock," a "dizzying disorientation brought on by the premature arrival of the future."[4] This sense of technological "jet lag" has begun to affect people of all ages. Children and adolescents, for example, have often felt intensified pressure to grow up faster and achieve more. Dr. David Elkind observes that there are many "hurried children" today, those who are pressured to become adults before their time. Clothing styles, hairstyles, and tastes in music also frequently suggest this pressure to grow up rapidly.

## Economic Realities

In recent decades, we have witnessed major economic changes. By the mid 1980s, the pressure of less buying power, higher interest rates and inflation has created enormous stresses for many families. Until recently, unemployment remained in the double digits as well.

As a result, between a quarter and a third of American children are living in families experiencing great financial strain and suffering from basic deprivations.

Even more startling, at least three million children live in families whose incomes are less than $5000.

A related fact is that approximately one-third of all children in our society do not receive adequate health care. Among 42 nations keeping comparable statistics, the United States ranks 16th in infant mortality.

## Relational Transitions

Not only are there major external pressures such as technological change and economic realities, but there are also extensive internal changes within family relationships being experienced today. Such statistics as the following give witness to these changes:

- Despite the fact that 90–95% of adults eventually marry, there has been a 16-fold increase in the divorce rate in recent decades. By the early 1980s, there had been at least one million divorces annually, double the reported breakups in 1966, and nearly three times that of 1950. Approximately one in every three marriages will eventually end in divorce.
- It is estimated that 4 out of 10 children born in the 1970s will spend part of their childhoods in single-parent families, usually with the mother as the head of the household.
- Despite the high divorce rates, 80% of divorced persons eventually do remarry.
- An increasing number of mothers are returning to the work market. Today, more than 50% of mothers of school-age children and 40% of those with preschool-age children are working outside the home.

One of the major factors affecting the circumstance of family living is a redefinition of male and female sex roles. There has been increasing discussion about the similarities and differences which exist between males and females. Many of the old generalizations—men should hide their feelings, women are the "weaker sex," and so on—have proven to be inadequate.

And many of the traditional divisions of responsibility—women take care of the inside of the home, men take care of the outside, for example—have also proven to be unnecessary and outmoded.

But as we eliminate many of the old guidelines and models, we may find ourselves without clear guidelines for how to act in relationships. If men and women are truly equals today, what does that mean, for example, for their relationships in terms of dating? In decision-making processes? Regarding attitudes and habits in expressing affection? Earning a living? In managing a home?

An aspect of these relational transitions, as well as the pressure to grow up faster, is the increased sexual activity today experienced by both young men and women. Research done by the Allan Guttmacher Institute indicates that by age 19, four-fifths of the males and two-thirds of the females have participated in sexual intercourse. Furthermore, approximately one-half of all births outside of marriage and one-third of abortions happen to teenage mothers. Perhaps what is even more startling is this prediction by the Guttmacher Institute: If current trends continue, 4 out of every 10 girls will become pregnant at least once during their adolescent years.[5]

## Psychological Pressures

All of these changes, transitions, and advances have undoubtedly created enormous stresses for many families. Toffler notes that, traditionally, families have been society's "giant shock absorber"—the place to which people return after days filled with frustration and conflict. For many, families have remained a stable anchor in a stormy sea of change—at least that is what they want.

Now it appears that this flexible institution we call the family has itself been stretched to the breaking point. Note these trends:

- Approximately one out of four hospital beds is currently occupied by mental patients. And 10% of our population will be hospitalized for mental illness during their lifetime.

- Alcohol and drugs continue to be misused in epidemic proportions by millions of persons as ways to cope with stress. Significant increases in the incidence of eating disorders are another indication of the psychic pain people are experiencing.
- Reports of child abuse and neglect are increasing at a startling rate of 30% annually. Government sources such as the U.S. National Center on Child Abuse and Neglect estimate that there are at least one million abused and neglected children in our society. Some researchers feel that the actual numbers may be more than double these figures, because of the high number of cases that go unreported.
- There is an epidemic of violence between parents and children, and between spouses as well. Estimates of wives being abused by their husbands vary from a low of three million to a high of 40 million.

  Even more depressing is the reality that family conflicts account for one-fourth of all murders in our society. A recent California study shows that 52% of all women killed in that state met their deaths at the hands of a husband or lover.
- The suicide rate among children and youth has increased dramatically in recent years. For adolescents, suicide has become the second most frequent cause of death (after auto accidents).

It is no wonder then that as Toffler predicted, families who had traditionally been "giant shock absorbers" have felt severe shocks themselves. Spiralling divorce rates, changing roles and expectations, and other changes have resulted at times in feelings of confusion, disorientation, and frustration.

## Moral Perplexities

With these impending transitions, perhaps we should not be surprised that there are many new moral questions with which we are forced to struggle. Not only is there concern about whether or not there is life after death (a theology of eternal life), but also about when life begins and ends.

For example, families may find themselves confronted with the reality of an unwanted teenage pregnancy. Painful choices are involved when thinking of whether to keep the baby, give it up for adoption, or whether abortion is an acceptable alternative.

Recent statistics point to the widespread nature of these perplexities[6]:

- In the past few years, 20% of pregnancies in our society have been terminated by abortion.
- In some cities (such as Washington, D.C.), and states (such as New York), there have actually been more abortions than live births in recent years, according to a 1978 study.

A number of other perplexing issues with moral implications have also emerged. Issues such as artificial insemination, birth control, and euthanasia continue to be hotly debated in many quarters of our church and society.

## Church Tradition

During this time of rather startling development for families, where has the church been? How have some of its developing traditions impacted families?

- *Theologically,* there has been a primary focus on a faith that is quite personal and private. A related assumption often expressed is that if the church helps individuals, then families will automatically be helped as well. While this kind of ministry to individuals may be essential, we cannot automatically assume that family relationships are directly strengthened through this approach. There are people who may feel that they have a close relationship with God who may find it difficult to be a loving spouse or nurturing parent. For faith to be complete, its relational component must be activated as well (see James 2:14ff; 1 Corinthians 13).

- *Organizationally,* the church has developed over the years with many different programs for various groups of people. With much of church programming set up for age levels (children, youth, adults, and so on), there may be little thought about programming for family relationships, or the impact the "age level" approach to ministry will have on family life.

What may appear to be for families (such as "family worship") is often quite adult-oriented. Children and youth often feel they should "endure" these happenings and consequently develop negative attitudes about what they perceive to be irrelevant.

• *Educationally,* the church has most often modeled itself after the public school, in which classes are organized by age levels.

Age level learning may be appropriate for cognitive or intellectual learning, and in terms of developing relationships with peers. Yet such an approach does not deal as effectively with such areas as the affective (feelings) and behavioral (actions). Learning in these latter two areas can often be effectively done in an intergenerational setting, whether in groups of nuclear families, or in settings which involve people of all ages—young and old, single and married.

• *Strategically,* energy devoted to "family ministry" has most frequently been crisis-oriented—providing counseling services for those who need help with family problems. Such an approach is fashioned after the traditional approach to medicine and medical practice: to provide help for people who feel sick.

One of the difficulties with this approach to family ministry is that many people may not seek the help they need until it is too late. Often a concern about "saving face" or being "respectable" can stultify efforts to get help.

## Church and Families

No doubt, much of this more passive approach to families in the church has not been intended to hurt families. Rather, ministry has been based on an approach to ministry which focuses more exclusively on individuals and their relationship with God, than upon the network of relationships in which they live.

Perhaps as never before, the church needs to be a place of renewal and support for families. The church cannot be just another demand for our time, energy, and money or its ministry may be ignored or avoided. There are many stresses and changes which can cause people to be less tolerant of what is less than relevant. A sense of loyalty alone will not keep most people tied into the church.

As families feel loved, supported, and encouraged, their faith will become more practical and meaningful. Whatever strategies the church adopts for strengthening families, its investment of resources will pay rich dividends in terms of both family stability and church growth.

The church is a natural setting for learning how to grow and change. Theologically, we can build a strong case for a faith which continues to grow and develop throughout the life cycle (see Eph. 3:14-21, for example).

The challenge is to devise strategies for strengthening families— strategies which are integral to our faith, as well as relevant and adaptable to family needs. Since there is such a variety of family forms and needs, our approaches must be flexible.

### The Family and Its Life Cycle

A number of trends, both external and internal, have affected family functioning. Such factors can certainly have either positive or negative effects on the family's ability to relate and cope.

Another major factor which influences family functioning is based on the idea of family systems. Just as each individual person has a unique personality, so each family develops unique patterns of interaction which are based on the relationship of its members. These patterns of interaction maintain a sense of equilibrium or balance when confronted by stresses or changes. (See the next section for a discussion of unhealthy and healthy patterns of family functioning.)

Not only is this family system greatly influenced by the quality of interaction and other factors brought by each person, but the family system has its own developmental history, including periods of dynamic change, as well as intervals of relative calm.

Just as each individual grows and develops through successive changes (such as puberty, mid-life transition, retirement, and so on), so each family has a life cycle with predictable periods. And each individual's development affects and interacts with the life cycle of the family. (See RM 1, "The Family Life Cycle.")

Truly, within families, no person is an island. Even though persons may experience growth and change in their own unique ways, they will also influence their families and be influenced by them.

## Family Wellness: A Focus for Ministry

### Personal Health

Over the centuries there has traditionally been more concern about dealing with illnesses than with enhancing health. The development of both medicine and psychology was rooted in a preoccupation with illness, whether physical or emotional, and its eradication.

We know that persons are physically ill when they exhibit pain, discomfort or do not feel very well. Frequently, medicine can help persons by taking away the pain or easing the discomfort. But it does not necessarily make a person well.

Some of the illnesses which are more emotionally based are depression, severe anxiety, neuroses and psychosis. Again, a person can get competent counseling which can help relieve some of the symptoms of emotional distress. But counseling alone does not necessarily make a person emotionally well.

Health, then, is much more than the absence of illness. The latter is merely a state of being neither sick nor well. Health, on the other hand, is a positive, assertive stance toward life; it is a feeling of vitality, of well-being, of being in control. It is seeking to fulfill one's potential in all areas of life, including the physical, emotional, social, moral, and spiritual dimensions. Health is active rather than passive, focusing more on potentials than on deficits.

Jesus Christ challenged people to aim toward being whole or mature (see Matt. 5:48). More recently, Abraham Maslow described such healthy persons as self-actualizing, while Carl Rogers described them as fully functioning.

Recently, Gail Sheehy conducted a fascinating survey among several thousand persons who had been identified as happy and successful in life. She concluded that there were a number of qualities which were shared by such persons, including a sense of direction in life, successful coping with life transitions, satisfying relationships, and a positive point-of-view. Her conclusions, then, support the notion that well-being is more than the absence of illness or pathology; it is positive, vigorous, and a potential which every human being has.[7]

A life-style of wellness, then, not only helps persons reduce the incidence of illness or disease. It provides them with greater meaning and purpose, as well as deeper satisfaction, in living.

## Family Dysfunctions

There is a parallel development of interest in what constitutes family wellness. Just as personal well-being is more than the absence of illness, so family wellness is more than the absence of dysfunctions or problems.

In the past several decades, significant research has been done on various aspects of family difficulties. We know that in a troubled family, there is a lack of harmony, often expressed in either extreme of emotional estrangement, or in a suffocating enmeshment in which people are not known as individuals.

In such "closed" families, as family therapist Virginia Satir calls them, there is little concern for the welfare or esteem of its members, but rather a focus on their performance. Communication patterns are poor. There may be either withdrawal in which people do not communicate directly, or there may be constant badgering, attacking or blaming.

Dysfunctional families usually resist change and unconsciously do not want to get well. Unresolved problems and tensions mark their relationship.

To deal with the variety of family dysfunctions, there are a great variety of approaches to family therapy, most of them designed to help families diminish their dysfunctions.

## Qualities of Healthy Families

Until recently family research has not focused on identifying the qualities of the strong or healthy families. But now such research does exist. There is a burgeoning interest in what constitutes family well-being.

Some of the most seminal research has been conducted by Dr. Nick Stinnett and his associates at the University of Nebraska at Lincoln. A study of hundreds of families has uncovered several important characteristics of strong families.[8] Dr. Stinnett defines family strengths as

> Those relationship patterns, interpersonal skills and competencies, and social and psychological characteristics which create a sense of positive family identity, promote satisfying and fulfilling interaction among family members, encourage the development of the potential of the family group and individual family members, and contribute to the family's ability to deal effectively with stress and crises.[9]

Another helpful study conducted by Dolores Curran has found 15 specific traits in healthy families.[10]

The qualities these researchers have identified can be grouped into the following categories:

## 1. Appreciation

Healthy families appreciate each other. There is a supportive, affirming environment in such families. The family group together and each of its individual members are appreciated and loved. Thus, even though there is a strong bond of togetherness, there is also great respect for the privacy and individual concerns of each family member.

## 2. Time

The use of time is an important concern in the healthy family. Time together as families is an important priority, both in terms of its quality and its quantity. Despite the pressures which can drive family members apart, healthy families make concerted efforts to eat together as regularly as possible and share leisure times together as well.

Since such families appreciate each other, there is enjoyment in play as well as in the more serious aspects of living.

## 3. Communication

The communication patterns of the healthy family are an important concern. Communication is direct, loving and constructive. Persons take responsibility for expressing their feelings but work hard at listening to the feelings and needs of others as well.

Since each person is appreciated as an important part of the family, the feelings of each person are expressed and understood by the others.

## 4. Commitment

Healthy families possess a strong sense of togetherness, a commitment to stay related even during times of transition, difficulty, or crisis. There is a feeling of mutual trust, a shared sense of responsibility in which each family member feels involved. Yet this bond of togetherness is not so overbearing that it stifles the individual growth and development of each of its members.

This sense of commitment also guides the family in the development and enjoyment of family traditions, times of celebration or commemoration which have special meaning for the family.

## 5. Faith

Healthy families generally seem to have a solid core of moral and spiritual beliefs as well. There is concern about the rightness or wrongness of actions, and for how actions will impact other people. Values such as empathy as well as serving others are made a priority. Serving and loving God is also of great importance.

Thus, healthy families do not become emotional or relational islands. They value involvement with other persons and profit from the support and encouragement which such involvement can bring.

## 6. Crisis Management

The goal in healthy families is not to avoid crisis or pain, but to deal with difficulties in positive and constructive ways. There is a bond of interdependence in strong families which helps them through transitions or difficulties which can tear apart more dysfunctional families.

Yet the approach to crisis in the healthy family is not one of rigidity but adaptability. There is a flexibility in confronting life which encourages the creative resolution of conflicts. Rules for dealing with conflict are both realistic and clear.

Healthy families seem to get stronger as a result of coping with life. Their stress management skills are such that the bond of togetherness becomes stronger and more vibrant throughout the life cycle.

## Family Wellness and Ministry

There is no doubt that we need to find creative ways to help families overcome their dysfunctions. Through individual, marital, family, and group counseling, persons who seek to make their family lives better need to find places where such opportunities are available. And the church is one alternative for the providing of such services.

But at the same time, we have an opportunity as perhaps never before to help build healthy families—to help them not only overcome their dysfunctions or illnesses, but also to become truly strong and healthy.

Especially in a time when family relationships are experiencing so many changes, when there is ongoing dialog about how to even define what a family is, we have an unparalleled opportunity to develop a ministry with families with a special focus on family wellness.

Undoubtedly, to make such a ministry a priority is to take a step of faith and courage. Families are not necessarily waiting for these efforts. Such attempts will be costly, not only in terms of money, but in terms of training persons to provide leadership for these ministries.

But to make family ministry a focal point of what a local church is all about is to be on the growing edge of what is needed today as well as for generations to come.

## A Time for Advocacy

There is a growing awareness throughout our society that in order for families to both survive and thrive, there needs to be a core of persons deeply committed to family welfare who will serve as advocates for families. Without family advocates in society, there would be no legislation which seeks to eliminate some of the socioeconomic, political, social and psychological hurdles to healthy family functioning. There would be no consciousness raising about the needs which families have. There would be little dialog about how families are changing and why they are still so vital for healthy personal and interpersonal growth and development.

This same kind of advocacy is needed within the church at large, as well as within each local congregation. People are needed who see a ministry with families as a mission, as an opportunity and responsibility which will involve the investment of personal gifts and resources.

Without such advocates in our congregations, programs will continue to develop which can inadvertently add more strain on families, often just because of the additional time pressures and competition for precious family time.

With such advocacy, there can be a concerted, coordinated effort to evaluate what is currently being done within a local congregation and community, as well as mapping short-range and long-range goals for building a strong family ministry.

And that brings us to the next section, a plan for developing the leadership and strategies which are needed for such a vital ministry.

# PART TWO
# IMPLEMENTATION

## Introduction

At this point, a person may agree that family ministry is essential in light of the needs of families today, and that the church needs to be relevant in its ministry.

But knowing where to begin can seem overwhelming. When considering how over-organized and over-programmed many churches already are, where does one begin to strategize for family ministry?

In this section, we will provide an overview of how to get started, as well as how to develop the leadership essential for this important endeavor.

No matter which options are selected, we need to remember that the fundamental assumption upon which family ministry is based is that every individual person, couple, and family possess the potential for further development of their well-being and their relationships. We all can continue to grow throughout the life cycle. And this growth process can be expedited by marriage and family enrichment programs offered through the ministry of the local church.

## Strategizing for Family Ministry: An Overview

### Options for Consideration

In getting started with planning ways to implement a ministry with families, we can provide a framework of various options for consideration. A person need not feel that all of these options should be selected and implemented at once. Rather, a careful process of deliberation can guide persons to develop a strategy which will be most effective and meaningful in their particular situation. It is essential to begin in the areas in which there is the greatest evident need.

There are a great number of options which are often included in family ministry. (*Note:* Refer to RM 2, "Family Ministry through the Life Cycle," for an overview of how family ministry is related to various phases of the family life cycle.)

## *Preparation for Marriage*

The joys of marriage can be maximized and problems minimized when the church takes seriously its mission to prepare people for the marriage relationship.

Such preparation really needs to take place throughout the life cycle. To wait until a couple has announced its engagement may not allow enough time or opportunity to deal with some of the potential concerns or difficulties.

For this reason, preparation for marriage should include the following components:

1. *Relationship education* can be provided for children, youth, and adults as a means of helping people sharpen their communication and relational skills. Learning to communicate, listen, and care is essential for building healthy relationships.

2. *Sexuality education* is needed so that people of all ages can develop a Christian understanding of human sexuality. Through participation in open discussions, such positive attitudes and responsible behaviors can develop.

The church may want to consider sponsoring a special workshop for parents on how to help children deal with their sexuality, as well as with any special concerns they may have as parents. Children are more likely to develop positive and responsible attitudes if their parents have such positive attitudes themselves.

For children and youth, a special learning experience could be led by members of the pastoral staff, doctors, counselors, and other such persons. Such workshops should be offered at least once a year and geared to the age of the people involved. If desired, parents could be included in these workshops as well.

3. *Premarital counseling* can be an essential step for promoting marital wellness. Whether provided in a small group setting or for individual couples, a structured series which deals with issues such as intimacy, sexuality, communication, finances, and roles and expectations can be a helpful start for couples.

Consider providing at least two of the sessions after couples have been married for a few weeks (the neomarital period). At that time, the questions and concerns will have become much more specific than they may have been before the wedding.

Also consider developing a support-discussion group of couples about to be married, newlyweds, as well as couples who have been married for some time. Such a group can be an ongoing source of encouragement during this vital time of transition and adjustment.

## Marriage Enrichment

With all of the strains and changes couples are experiencing today, the church needs to provide experiences which will strengthen marriages and help couples develop greater intimacy and commitment. David and Vera Mace, in their book *Marriage Enrichment in the Church,* note that the church needs to help people realize "the latent potentiality in the relationship for the deepening of love, trust, and mutual understanding and support."[1]

In order for there to be healthy family life in the two parent family, there needs to be a happy, growing marriage as well. Keeping a proper balance between the pressures and demands of parenting and the need for a strong marital relationship is one of the greatest challenges a couple will face in their family experience.

There are a variety of ways in which the church can enhance marriage relationships:

1. *A marriage enrichment retreat* provides couples with time away from other family pressures to focus on their marriage. Whether held at the church facility itself or at a nearby camp or conference grounds, such retreats have been found to be a valuable experience for thousands of couples. (*Note:* See the following section for a specific retreat design.)

2. *A couples' growth group* can be organized as a Sunday morning elective adult class, a weeknight support group, and so on. Such

groups can begin with an initial four- to six-week commitment, at which time they can evaluate whether or not they would like to continue.

## Parent Education

One of the greatest challenges of life is being a nurturing parent to children and adolescents. Family therapist Virginia Satir describes parenting in this way:

> I regard this as the hardest, most complicated, anxiety-ridden, sweat and blood-producing job in the world. It requires the ultimate in patience, common sense, commitment, humor, tact, love, wisdom, awareness, and knowledge. At the same time, it holds the possibility for the most rewarding, joyous experience of a lifetime.[2]

The home and church need to be partners in the nurturing of people of all ages. Christian nurture and the development of values should not be relegated exclusively to the church. It is a process which needs to take place at home as well.

Parents often may feel overwhelmed at the responsibilities and expectations of parenthood, not only when children are first born, but also throughout the years of childhood and adolescence. The church can provide an exciting ministry when it supports and cares for parents in their vital role as nurturers.

There are a number of ways in which parent education can be provided:

1. *An elective adult education class or workshop* can focus on the needs and concerns of parenting.

2. *Participation in community learning opportunities* will be enhanced as you inform parents of these workshops and seminars.

3. *A support group* of parents can provide opportunities for parents to share their concerns and pray for each other. Such groups can use a book on parenting for study. They can be organized by the age level of their children in groups which cross over the various age levels.

4. *Special learning experiences* for mothers, fathers, or single parents on a weeknight or Saturday morning can focus on these special interests and concerns.

## Family Enrichment

We have already used the word "family" in a number of ways—as the "family" or people of God; as an "extended family"—whether actual families with all of their relatives, or groups which include various age levels and singles and marrieds within the church.

In this context, we are talking about nuclear families—in which there are one or two parents, along with at least one child.

Special enrichment opportunities can enhance their family relationships. (*Note:* See the following section for several specific models.)

Among the options for enriching nuclear families are the following:

1. *A family retreat*—an opportunity to focus on family relationships in a setting away from home pressures.

2. *A family workshop*—a single event or short series of workshops on selected family topics, such as communication, self-esteem, values, and such.

3. *Family clusters*—a small group of families who meet for informal fellowship, sharing and learning. The group decides how long the cluster will meet. (*Note:* Family clusters can also be based on the "Extended Family" model.)

4. *Special events*—such as "Dads and Kids" fun nights, or a mother-daughter event can be other ways to enhance family relationships. (*Note:* Be sensitive to the fact that not all families will have fathers or mothers available. Be sure that events are structured so that everyone feels comfortable attending.)

## Intergenerational Ministry

Intergenerational ministry, which involves two or more generations together, may include several possibilities:

1. *Worship* can be restructured to acknowledge the presence of children and youth, as well as adults. Special components, such as a children's sermon or the use of a youth choir, as well as gearing the worship language so that it is understandable to all ages, are essential. (Option: Occasional special worship experiences which

are more informally and intentionally intergenerational can provide a good first step.)

2. *"Extended family"* groups are groups of people who may not be related formally but through their common faith. Children, youth, and adults (including singles and couples, young as well as middle-age or older adults) may be included in such groups. They may be organized for fellowship, worship, study, or service. "Extended family" groups may be organized for a limited series of sessions (such as six to eight get-togethers), or for an indefinite length of time.

3. *Special programs* are special events, usually a single event, such as a family Christmas program, or a series of specific duration, such as an Advent or Lenten series. Such events are planned to include people of all ages.

Notice that all of these intergenerational ministries cover the entire family life cycle.

## Singles Ministry

Many churches incorporate a ministry with single people within family ministry. Specific ministries may involve unmarried persons in at least two different ways:

1. *Special programs for single persons*—workshops, support groups, and fellowship get-togethers related to the special interests and needs of single persons.

2. *Programs which seek to bring single and married persons, young and old, together*—groups such as "extended family" groups, intergenerational worship, and so on.

Such a ministry often includes special efforts with the formerly married—persons who find themselves single again and coping with the adjustments of a new life-style. Workshops and support groups which meet for sharing and encouraging one another can provide a link of a concern to those who often feel left out of other aspects of church ministry.

## Family Counseling

Despite the focus on the enhancement of family wellness, there is undoubtedly still a great need for providing counseling services for individuals, couples, and families who are struggling with difficulties. Persons cannot accentuate the positive and fulfill their potential until they are able to deal with some of the emotional or relational blocks or situational difficulties which have made them focus on pain and discomfort.

There are a number of strategies for providing family counseling:

1. *Referrals* to professionals in the community who can competently handle such situations.

2. *Crisis intervention* by the pastoral staff or trained lay persons.

3. *Pastoral counseling* by members of the church staff.

4. *Professional counseling* by one or more licensed persons hired by the church to provide such services.

## Getting Started

It is important for a church to move slowly and plan carefully, so that family ministry does not become another "flash in the pan" but rather can endure and excel.

Here are a number of suggestions for getting started:

● *Help the church develop a family awareness.*
  Help the congregation to understanding the importance of families. Guide church leadership to evaluate what is already being done in terms of family ministry and what should be started. (*Note:* See the section on leadership development for a specific plan.)

● *Do personal study on family life.*
  Whether you are a clergyperson or layperson, you will be able to speak and share from a stronger position of understanding if your reading on family life is current.

● *Guide church leadership in study.*
  Ask that church leaders take turns reading a book on marriage and family life and then presenting a brief review at a board meeting.

● *Have resources available for the congregation.*
  Be sure that your church library has an ample section of books, tapes, magazines, and other resources on marriage and family life.

- *Develop a Family Ministry Task Force to oversee the development of this important ministry.*
  Such a task force may include current church leaders, but it could also involve several people from the congregation who have an interest in families and their development. Be sure to invite children and young people to be a part of this task force as well. (*Note:* See the section on leadership development for a specific plan.)
- *Plan informal intergenerational activities.*
  Offer special events such as an intergenerational workshop or fellowship experience. Summer, for example, is often a time when other activities have shut down for several weeks. This can be an excellent time to offer something new and exciting.

# Leadership Development

## Introduction

If a ministry with families is going to flourish, it will need strong, creative leadership—those who will be willing to advocate the use of church money and time for such efforts, as well as those who can provide leadership for specific events.

With all of the pressures and obligations which the clergy staff experiences, it is important that the leadership responsibility be shared. In addition to interested laypersons in your congregation, consider involving other people from your community, such as teachers and counselors, to assist with any leadership needs you may have.

## General Church Leadership: Developing Family Awareness

No matter how large your church staff is, one of the long-range goals in family ministry is the involvement of laypersons who may function in either a leadership, supportive, or participatory role. Without this involvement, family ministry can easily be seen as a special project of interest only to the clergy or of a special interest group, and not of any great relevance to the congregation at large.

An essential step for building a family ministry within a congregation is to develop family awareness among the current leadership. The following outline for a 90-minute leadership training experience is intended to raise consciousness regarding what is currently happening in family ministries in your congregation.

Be sure that copies of your church bulletin for a typical month, as well as your church's last annual report, and current operating budget, are available for participants.

You may want to schedule this event during a regular leadership meeting, or at a special session.

## Workshop Design

### 1. Get Acquainted (10 minutes)

After a brief overview of the workshop's purpose and an opening prayer, divide into groups of three or four. Ask persons to share one or two times in their growing up years when their families benefited from the ministry of your church. If their families were not active in the church, how could they have benefited from such ministry?

### 2. Input (15 minutes)

You or an appointed leader should be prepared to present a brief overview of the importance of the family and how various trends have affected family life. Be sure to present an introduction to family wellness as well. Distribute copies of RM 1 and RM 2 (*Note:* See "Foundational Concerns" section for resources.)

### 3. Evaluation (45 minutes)

Distribute copies of RM 3, "An Evaluation Tool for Developing Family Awareness," as well as copies of your current bulletins, annual report, and budget.

As a group, work through the process of reviewing your calendar and budget and evaluating their impact on families. (*Option:* Complete this process in groups of four to six: spend the last 10 minutes sharing thoughts and insights together in the large group.)

Encourage a spirit of openness and objectivity in this process. Be aware that there probably will not be unanimous feelings or opinions in these discussions. Reassure people that a number of good things may already be happening, and that the goal of this process is to strengthen what is already happening.

This discussion and evaluation process can help your leaders deepen their understanding of how important family relationships are and the impact of current church programming on these relationships.

*4. Planning (15 minutes)*

Guide the group to consider what the next steps should be in strengthening a ministry with families. The goal should be that a small group task force take on the responsibility of developing this ministry (if another group has not already been assigned this responsibility).

There are several options regarding membership on this task force:

- Several members of your current board.
- A group of persons currently responsible for the educational ministry of your congregation.
- A task force of persons who may not currently be involved in leadership. You may want to recruit couples or families as well as individuals for this group.

Decide together who will be responsible for recruiting and organizing this leadership group, as well as the process through which they will make decisions, the money available through the budget, and other critical factors. Designate someone to coordinate the first meeting of the task force.

*5. Wrap-Up (5 minutes)*

Conclude this workshop with prayer. Ask several volunteers to express thanks to God for families, and to ask for a deepened commitment to a meaningful ministry with families.

## Family Ministries Task Force: Leadership Enhancement

Once the task force leadership has been identified and recruited, the next step of strategizing and planning for specific family ministries can be taken. Remember that children and youth, as well as adults, can make valuable contributions in this planning venture.

What follows is an outline for several planning sessions. Because of the nature of this group, a potluck meal will help create a warm, informal environment in which the planning process would be enhanced and relationships deepened. The "Get Acquainted" activities will guide group members to a greater understanding and appreciation of each other.

These sessions could be scheduled on a weekly basis.

## Session 1: The Importance of Families

*1. Get Acquainted (15–20 minutes)*

Take time to get acquainted. Divide into groups of two. Have the pairs interview each other to discover what is of interest to each other. Then have the pairs introduce each other to the rest of the group.

*2. Brainstorming (10–15 minutes)*

As a group, develop two lists:

• Why families are important.

• How families today are changing.

Record group thoughts on newsprint or chalkboard.

*3. Review of the "Developing Family Awareness" Workshop (10–15 minutes)*

Have someone who attended the church leadership workshop on family awareness sum up their findings regarding the impact of the current ministry of the church with families. A summary of what is already being provided for families, as well as any general feelings regarding the future of family ministry in your congregation, should also be shared.

*4. Sharing and Praying (20–30 minutes)*

Aim to make your task force a support group where individual and family needs can be shared and prayed for. This can be done in groups of two or three or in the larger group, depending on your group size.

An important goal on the task force is that the qualities of family wellness which have been described will be experienced within the task force as well.

## Session 2: Family Wellness

*1. Get Acquainted (15–20 minutes)*

In groups of two, reminisce about a special family happening during the past year or two. What happened? What made these experiences so special? Then share another time which was more stressful or difficult. What made this experience so stressful?

*2. Brainstorming (15–20 minutes)*

Mention that the task force is going to be developing strategies for helping families become strong and well. Work together to develop a list of what healthy families are like. You may want to begin with the qualities discussed in the "Foundational Concerns" section. Distribute copies of RM 4 "Qualities of a Healthy Marriage and Family." Ask group members to think of situations in which a family might find it difficult to exhibit each quality.

*3. Sharing and Praying (30–40 minutes)*

In groups of three or four, compare the qualities of the family of your growing up years with the qualities of family wellness just listed. In what areas was each family strong? Weak? Are there any lingering sources of pain or resentment from those growing up years? Pray together about these concerns.

## Session 3: Consulting with Families

*1. Get Acquainted (15–20 minutes)*

In small groups, reminisce about what family traditions each person had in the growing up years. Any special family get-togethers? Any special holiday celebrations? How were birthdays celebrated? How did these traditions make family life special?

*2. Family Survey Development (30–40 minutes)*

Work together to develop a family survey. On chalkboard or newsprint, list questions you want to ask people in your church community. Questions should be concise and need only a brief response, for tabulation purposes. Be sure that such concerns as these are included:

● The age groupings in your congregation (how many preschoolers, elementary age, young people, young adults, middle-age, the aging, and so on).

- The family relationships (the number of single persons, couples without children, two-parent families, single-parent families, people living alone and so on).
- Family needs and interests (what kind of events on what kinds of topics would people like the church to sponsor).

*3. Family Survey Distribution (5–10 minutes)*

Take a few minutes to make plans for how the survey will be distributed, collected, and tabulated. Some options:

- Have parishioners complete the survey in a worship service or during Sunday school classes.
- Mail the surveys to all constituents. Ask that people return them the following Sunday or by a specific date.

*4. Sharing and Prayer (20–30 minutes)*

Continue the process of meeting in small groups for sharing and praying together.

## Session 4: The Needs of Families

*1. Get Acquainted (15–20 minutes)*

Distribute lumps of modeling clay or playdough to participants. Ask them to mold a shape which represents a strong feeling they experienced during the previous week. Then go around the group and share what the shapes represent.

If time permits, ask participants to make a second shape that symbolizes something that happened in their family experience recently (either with their parents, relatives, or in their current family). Then go around the group again so that everyone has an opportunity to share.

*2. Family Survey Tabulation (30–60 minutes)*

In small congregations, you may be able to tabulate the survey results in your task force meeting. (*Option:* Have persons designated by the task force tabulate the results and bring a report of the findings to this meeting.)

*3. Discussion (10–15 minutes)*

Make a list together of the most urgent family needs in your congregation, based on your survey results. What are the areas of greatest interest for ministry? Introduce RM 2, "Family Ministry Through the Life Cycle."

*4. Sharing and Praying (20–30 minutes)*

Continue the process of meeting in small groups for sharing and praying together.

## Session 5: Planning for Ministry

*1. Get Acquainted (15–20 minutes)*

Divide into groups of two or three. Ask participants to think of at least one dream they had when they were younger—something they wanted to do, a job they wanted to have, and so on. Did this dream come true? Why or why not? What is a dream people have for themselves for the future?

*2. Review of Needs (5–10 minutes)*

Refer to the list of needs that was developed at the last session. Now that the group has had time to reflect on all of this, are there any changes in this list that participants would like to make?

*3. Planning (30–40 minutes)*

Now it is time to plan for what is actually going to take place in family ministry in your congregation.

Complete the following steps:

- *Prioritizing.* Look through the list of needs and interests. Work together to prioritize what is most urgent, what can wait until next year, what can be postponed for future consideration, and so on. Affix a number, beginning with number one for most urgent, next to each item.
- *Long-Range Planning.* Set some goals you would like to accomplish in the next five years (such as to develop support groups). Then identify the steps that will need to be completed in order for these five-year goals to be accomplished.
- *Implementing.* Identify together what programs or strategies will be implemented first. Be sure that the group refers to the "Models for Enhancing Family Wellness" section of this book for suggestions.
- *Delegating.* Decide who will do what for each event or program, what leadership needs there are, and so on.

*4. Sharing and Praying (20–30 minutes)*

In this final session of the planning phase for the task force, spend some time (either in small groups or in the large group) sharing what has been learned and experienced during these sessions. Trust all of these needs and concerns to God as the task force embarks on this exciting venture together.

## Subsequent Sessions

Once the strategies have been finalized and plans are set, an ongoing task force will still need to coordinate these efforts, and to evaluate their effectiveness. A session could be held monthly and include the following:

- Sharing and praying for each other and for the continuing efforts at family ministry.
- Updates on current happenings in family ministry (both descriptions and evaluations).
- Planning for future events.
- Reporting on books and other resources task force members have reviewed.

# PART THREE
# MODELS FOR ENHANCING FAMILY WELLNESS

## Introduction

Thus far, we have reviewed some foundational concerns regarding families and qualities that exemplify their wellness. We have discussed the importance of families and ways that the church can implement a significant ministry with them.

This section provides several specific workshops or programs, which can serve as the initial effort in the areas of marriage enrichment, parent education, and family enrichment.

In each of these areas, four 75–90 minute sessions are provided. They can be used in couples', parents', or intergenerational groups for four weekly sessions, or they can be incorporated into a weekend retreat setting. A weekend format would include the following schedule:

**Friday Evening**
    Arrival at the retreat site
    Session 1
**Saturday**
    Breakfast
    Session 2
    Break
    Session 3
    Lunch

Afternoon: Recreation/relaxation break
Dinner
Session 4
**Sunday**
Breakfast
Concluding Worship and Sharing
Cleanup/packing
Lunch
Head for home

No matter which format is selected, each of the workshops is designed to enhance one of the aspects of family wellness.

At the conclusion of each of the models, suggestions for other workshops and programs will be provided.

# A Model for Marriage Enrichment

## Objectives

These marriage enrichment workshops will enable the participants to:

- Reminisce about what initially attracted them to their spouses.
- List and describe several qualities of the healthy, growing marriage.
- Describe what can block a marriage from growing.
- Express what they especially appreciate about their spouses.
- Tell why both togetherness and separateness are essential for the growing marriage.
- Identify commonalities and differences couples see in their relationship.
- Reminisce about significant crises or difficulties couples have experienced and how these situations helped or hindered their relationship.
- Describe several important principles for handling conflicts effectively.
- Make plans for strengthening their marital relationships.

## Session 1: The Growing Marriage

*1. Get Acquainted (15–20 minutes)*

In small groups of four or six, have spouses describe how they met each other, and what it was that initially attracted them to each other. (*Option:* If you have a small group, do this sharing in one larger group.)

*2. Input (15–20 minutes)·*

Bc prepared to share the following with the couples:

- Introduce the series. Provide a brief overview of the objectives and activities for this workshop series. Share your enthusiasm and hope that this will be a meaningful and growing experience for each couple.
- Make a brief presentation of the qualities of the growing marriage. Distribute copies of RM 4, "Qualities of the Healthy Marriage and Family." As you prepare for this presentation, review the section on family wellness in the "Foundational Concerns" section of this book.

Briefly relate how each of these qualities is essential for the growing marriage:

Appreciation

Time

Communication

Commitment

Faith

Crisis management

If possible, relate a few significant personal experiences about these qualities.

*3. Small Group Discussion (15–20 minutes)*

Divide into groups of three, being sure that spouses are not in the same groups. Ask groups to brainstorm what can block a marriage from growing and what helps it to grow. Be sure they have sheets of paper and pencils for making lists.

### 4. Large Group Sharing (5–10 minutes)

Get back into the large group. Take a few minutes for each of the groups to share their lists. Develop a composite list on chalkboard or newsprint.

### 5. Affirmation Bombardment (10–15 minutes)

Ask that spouses sit together. Be sure that there is adequate space for each couple to talk privately.

Ask each couple to determine who will be person A and who will be person B.

Then ask that person A share with person B what he or she especially appreciates about the other person.

Person B then feeds back what she or he heard the spouse share. The process is then reversed, so that person A receives the affirmation and feeds back to person B what was expressed.

### 5. Wrap-Up (5 minutes)

Gather back in the large group. Mention how important it is to express appreciation to our spouses on a regular basis. Such sharing should be specific and relate to what the other spouse would especially like to hear.

Thank the group for their interest. Conclude with a time of fellowship and refreshments.

## Session 2: Building Bridges Instead of Walls

### 1. Get Acquainted (15–20 minutes)

Divide into several small groups of three or four. Ask participants to think of a couple they know who has a happy, growing marriage. What is it about such a couple that they especially admire? Share this information in the small groups.

### 2. Input (15–20 minutes)

As you begin, ask persons to list some of the qualities they had identified.

Mention that one of the important qualities of the growing marriage is that there be a balance between togetherness and separateness.

Talk about what each of these words means and why it is so essential:

- Togetherness (common goals, commitment to the relationship, some similar interests, similar values, and so on).
- Separateness (the freedom for each person to have an individual identity—in such ways as vocation, unique personality and temperament, different interests, and so on).

Give specific examples if possible.

### 3. Bridge Building Exercise (35–40 minutes)

Ask that the couples sit together. Distribute copies of RM 5 "Bridge Building Exercise." Guide them to identify what they have in common with each other, as well as ways in which they are different.

### 4. Wrap-Up (5–10 minutes)

Get together back in the large group. Summarize again the importance of learning to appreciate our differences, as well as ways in which we are similar to our spouses. We should avoid the temptation of pressuring our spouses to conform totally to each other, but instead seek to find a healthy balance between togetherness and separateness.

Conclude your session with a time of fellowship and refreshments.

## Session 3: Coping with Stress and Crisis

### 1. Get Acquainted (15–20 minutes)

Divide up into small groups of three or four. Having spouses in the same small groups is optional. Ask that persons reminisce about times of crisis they experienced in their families of origin. How was crisis or conflict handled? Did these times of difficulty serve to strengthen or estrange family members?

### 2. Large Group Discussion (10–15 minutes)

Once you are back in the large group, ask that participants list the typical stresses and crises which can occur in any marriage. List these ideas on chalkboard or newsprint.

### 3. Couple Sharing (15–20 minutes)

Ask that spouses sit together for this activity. Distribute copies of RM 6, "Marriage Time Line." Spouses should each complete the exercise alone and then compare their thoughts with each other. Then they should create a time line with which they both agree.

Acknowledge that these difficulties may often initiate times of most significant growth and change in a marriage.

### 4. Input (10–15 minutes)

Once couples have completed their time lines, get back together in the large group.

Share your thoughts on some basic principles for handling conflicts and crisis:

- Acknowledge that the conflict exists. (Sometimes people do not even agree that there is a conflict or crisis.)
- Identify the key points in the conflict.
- List alternatives for resolving the conflict.
- Evaluate, then prioritize the alternatives in their order of preference.
- Try the preferred alternative.
- When appropriate time has been allowed, evaluate the effectiveness of that alternative. (Should this plan of action continue, or should another alternative be attempted?)

Remind the couples that their relationship is more important than any conflict or crisis they may encounter. Acknowledge that some stresses never seem to go away and feel unresolvable.

Healthy communication skills and the willingness to compromise and be flexible are vital for handling stress. And there is often a need for confession of our frailties and errors to each other and for forgiveness.

### 5. Couple Sharing (10–15 minutes)

Ask that couples sit together for this activity. Ask that they identify a crisis or conflict they are facing currently in their relationship. If there is no current conflict, ask them to think of their most recent conflict. Guide them to plan ways to cope with this difficulty, using the guidelines you have presented in this session.

*6. Wrap-Up (5 minutes)*

When couples have completed their sharing, gather back in the large group. Mention again how important communication skills and flexibility are in handling stress, conflict and crisis. And perhaps the most important ingredient of all is the commitment to keep communicating and listening in the midst of those difficult times.

Conclude the session with a time of fellowship and refreshments.

## Session 4: Sharing Our Faith

*1. Small Group Discussion (10–15 minutes)*

Begin the session by dividing into several small groups. Make the groups consisting of nonspouses. Ask participants to identify what can make faith and religion a difficult or uncomfortable area for some couples and what makes it positive or comfortable for others.

*2. Large Group Sharing (5–10 minutes)*

Gather back in the large group. Have volunteers from each small group share their thoughts. Develop a composite list on chalkboard or newsprint.

*3. Input (10–15 minutes)*

Prepare a brief presentation about the importance of having a common belief and value system. (*Note:* See the books by Curran, Larson, and Stinnett listed in the Resources section for additional thoughts on this topic.) Identify several ways that such a common faith system can be beneficial to couples:

- Brings a sense of unity.
- Provides a common frame of reference for dealing with conflicts.
- Provides strength and insight in dealing with conflict and crisis.

If possible, share personal experiences which reinforce these basic ideas.

*4. Couple Sharing (20–25 minutes)*

Ask that spouses sit together for this activity. Distribute copies of RM 7, "A Marriage Inventory." Guide couples to use this worksheet to evaluate their marriages. Have persons complete the worksheet individually, and then compare responses with their spouses. Encourage partners to focus their discussion especially on any matters for which there seems to be a difference of opinion.

Distribute blank sheets of paper, envelopes, and pencils to the couples. Ask that each couple work together to write themselves a letter, stating what their goals are for their marriage in the coming year. After the couples have written their letters, they insert the letters in envelopes, seal them, and address the envelopes to themselves.

Then collect letters. (*Note:* In a few months, mail these letters to the couples as a reminder of the goals they had made for themselves in the workshop series.)

*5. Wrap-Up (10–15 minutes)*

Thank the participants for their involvement in this workshop series. Ask them to share what has been especially meaningful.

Distribute copies of "Resources for Couples" (RM 8). Encourage couples to read books and other resources that can enhance their relationships.

Conclude with thoughts on what other opportunities there will be for the couples (see "Next Steps" for suggestions).

## Next Steps

Consider offering at least one of the following series as a means for couples to keep growing in their marriages:

- *Couple Communication*—a 4-session, 12-hour basic course in communication and listening skills. Complete resources are available for leading such a program. Some degree of experienced leadership is essential.
- *Evening for Couples*—a 4-session program which developed out of the Marriage Encounter program, along with the creative design of Lyman Coleman. This program does not require experienced leadership but can usually be led by the couples themselves.

See the Resources section for details on these materials.

# A Model for Parent Education

## Objectives

These parent education workshops will enable participants to:
- Identify circumstances which can cause family relationships to be stressful.
- List and describe several qualities of family wellness.
- Set personal goals for promoting family wellness in their own families.
- Describe and evaluate several styles of parenting.
- Tell why modeling and imitation are vital aspects of parenting.
- Clarify how personal needs are sometimes in conflict with family needs.

## Session 1: What Makes a Family Healthy?

*1. Get Acquainted (15–20 minutes)*

Welcome all participants to this series of workshops. Be sure that everyone introduces themselves in the larger group.

Provide a brief overview of the topics to be covered in this series of parent education workshops. Ask participants to identify the age levels of their children.

Divide into small groups of three or four. Ask them to list circumstances which can cause family relationships to be stressful, and those which can cause family life to be satisfying and meaningful.

*2. Large Group Sharing (5–10 minutes)*

After the groups have completed their lists, get together again in the large group. Develop a composite list on chalkboard or newsprint based on the ideas shared from the small group discussion.

*3. Input (10–15 minutes)*

Distribute copies of RM 4, "Qualities of the Healthy Marriage and Family." Make a brief presentation of the qualities of the growing, healthy family. As you prepare for this presentation, review the section on family wellness in the "Foundational Concerns" section of this book.

Briefly relate how each of these qualities is essential for the growing family:

Appreciation

Time

Communication

Commitment

Faith

Crisis management

If possible, relate a few significant personal experiences about these qualities.

*4. Large Group Discussion (10–15 minutes)*

Ask group members to identify when each of these qualities is difficult to exhibit. You may want to list these ideas on chalkboard or newsprint.

*5. Personal Reflection (10–15 minutes)*

Distribute copies of RM 9, "When I Stop to Think About It. . . ." Guide participants to complete this brief inventory of their own family experiences. Encourage them to be open and honest with themselves in evaluating where they think their families are at this point.

*6. Small Group Sharing (10–15 minutes)*

Divide into groups of two or three. Ask group members to share their thoughts about their families, based on the previous activity. Encourage them to be supportive and encouraging with each other.

*7. Wrap-Up (5–10 minutes)*

Get back together in the large group again. Summarize the key thoughts of this session. Conclude with prayer. Thank God for this opportunity to learn and grow in the experience of being parents and families.

## Session 2: Styles of Parenting

*1. Get Acquainted (15–20 minutes)*

Divide into small groups of three or four. Ask participants to share what their experience with their parents was like in their growing up years. What style of leadership did their parents provide? How were conflicts handled?

## 2. Input (15–20 minutes)

Prepare a presentation on the styles of parenting. Begin by mentioning that there are several different styles of parenting. Research has found that there are three basic styles or kinds. (Distribute copies of RM 10, "Styles of Parenting," for participants to use as a point of reference.)

Here is a brief description of each basic style:

- *Authoritarian*—often rigid, overbearing, more concerned about obedience and conformity than with the quality of the parent-child relationship; does not allow participation in the decision-making process by the children.
- *Permissive*—often quite uninvolved emotionally; children usually have a great deal of freedom; little connectedness between parents and children.
- *Democratic*—encourages participation by children in the decision-making process, but parents still maintain a leadership role and are authoritative. There are still rules and structures.

## 3. Large Group Sharing (10–15 minutes)

While still in the large group, identify times when each style may be appropriate, and times when each style may be ineffective.

Again, mention that a person may at various times use all of these styles, but that there may be one predominant style.

## 4. Personal Reflection (10–15 minutes)

Distribute copies of RM 11, "Evaluating My Own Style of Parenting." Encourage participants to think about their own style of parenting and then to identify how they may want to change this style. How would they like to improve the way they relate to their children?

## 5. Small Group Sharing (10–15 minutes)

Divide into groups of two or three. Ask group members to share their thoughts and plans as related to styles of parenting. Encourage them to pray for each other as they seek to implement changes in family leadership this week.

## 6. Wrap-Up (5–10 minutes)

Reassemble in the large group. Summarize the key ideas presented in this session. Mention that the process of parenting—the style and way in which we relate to our children—is an important factor in indicating how healthy our families are.

Ask for a volunteer to conclude this session with prayer, asking God for guidance and wisdom and implementing changes in family relationships.

## Session 3: Modeling and Imitation

### 1. Get Acquainted (15–20 minutes)

Divide into groups of two or three. Ask group members to identify qualities (styles of leadership, values, and so on) of their parents which they have imitated, and qualities they have not imitated.

### 2. Input (10–15 minutes)

Make a brief presentation on the importance of modeling and imitation. Begin by reminiscing about the impact which your parents have had on your life—the qualities, styles, values, and so on, which you have tended to imitate, and those which you have not.

*The family: first place for learning values* (Acknowledge how important the early years of a child's life are, and how much children learn by watching and imitating their parents.)

Give specific examples of ways that children imitate their parents:

- Values

- Ways of relating to others

- Ways of handling feelings and conflicts

- Attitudes toward oneself

*The challenge of changing patterns* (Mention that once these early patterns are set, they are quite difficult, but not impossible, to change. A negative example can have as great an impact on children as can a positive example.)

### 3. Brainstorming (10–15 minutes)

Ask group members to identify the qualities they would like their children to imitate. Make a list of group ideas on chalkboard or newsprint.

### 4. Personal Reflection (10–15 minutes)

Distribute copies of RM 12, "Personally Speaking." Guide participants to take several minutes to reflect on their own family situations and to jot down their responses to the statements on the worksheet.

### 5. Small Group Sharing (10–15 minutes)

Ask that participants meet in small groups of two or three, as in previous sessions. You may want to divide the groups according to the age level of their children, by whether they are from single parent or two-parent families, and so on. Encourage participants to share their thoughts on the kind of examples they want to be for their children, and any changes they would like to initiate toward that end.

### 6. Wrap-Up (5–10 minutes)

Reassemble in the large group. Summarize the key ideas presented in this session. Reassure parents that there are a number of influences on their children's development, including the influence of other family members, friends, school teachers, and so on. Yet the influence of a healthy parent can make an indelible impression on the health of children and young people during years when they need healthy models.

Conclude with a time of prayer.

## Session 4: Commitment

### 1. Get Acquainted (15–20 minutes)

Divide into small groups of two or three. Give each group a sheet of paper and a pencil. Guide groups to write the letters of the word *"parenting"* along the left margin vertically. Ask them to think of qualities of effective parenting which begin with each of the letters of the word *"parenting."*

Then reassemble back in the large group. Ask a volunteer from each group to read the list of qualities they identified.

### 2. Input (10–15 minutes)

Focus on effective parenting as being a creative combination of nurturing family members while meeting one's own needs as well.

- *Nurturing family members* (describe how one nurtures—cares for, encourages, guides).
- *Meeting one's own needs* (developing as an adult, becoming fully functioning; acknowledging and working on personal growth).
- Share a few of your own experiences and frustrations on this issue, if you are a parent.
- *Commitment: a key ingredient* (mention how important a sense of commitment is to one's own family, as well as to one's own wellbeing).

### 3. Large Group Discussion (5–10 minutes)

While in the large group, think together of potential conflicts which may arise between personal and family needs (such as finances, different values, the need for space, and so on). Think together of ways to resolve each of these difficulties. What should persons do if these conflicts seem unresolvable?

### 4. Personal Reflection (10–15 minutes)

Distribute copies of RM 13, "Joys and Frustrations of Family Life." Encourage participants to reflect for several minutes about their personal needs and interests as they relate to family needs and interests. Guide them to complete the worksheet.

### 5. Small Group Sharing (10–15 minutes)

Divide into small groups of two or three, as in previous sessions. Encourage participants to share their thoughts regarding the potential conflicts between personal and family needs, and how a sense of commitment can help them resolve these conflicts.

### 6. Wrap-Up (5–10 minutes)

Acknowledge again how challenging it is to maintain a proper balance between meeting one's own needs, looking after the needs and interests of family members, as well as our involvement in the larger world. An important part of our faith is to love others and serve them, but not at the cost of our own integrity and self-esteem.

Distribute copies of RM 14, "Resources for Parents." Encourage participants to keep reading and growing.

Discuss any future parent education events which will be offered (see "Next Steps" section for suggestions).

Conclude with a time of prayer. Ask that several participants pray regarding personal and family concerns.

## Next Steps

Consider offering at least one of the following series as a means for parents to keep enhancing their skills as parents:

- *Systematic Training for Effective Parenting* (STEP) is an excellent series of learning experiences for parents. Complete resources are available and do not require experienced leadership for the workshops to be effective. Another program called STEP/TEEN has been developed for parents of adolescents.
- *Evenings for Parents* is a 4-session program which does not require experienced leadership. It provides a creative approach to the discussion of family concerns.
- *Parenting for Peace and Justice.* This excellent book relates parenting to a number of contemporary concerns, including justice, sexism, and world peace. A leader's guide is also available.
- *Active Parenting* is an innovative parent education program which includes the use of video presentations.

See the Resources section for complete details on these materials.

# A Model for Family Enrichment

## Objectives

These family enrichment workshops will enable participants to:
- Get acquainted with other families.
- Enjoy informal times of singing and sharing.
- Make plans for spending quality time together in their families.
- Express appreciation to each family member.
- Describe, role play, and evaluate several patterns of communication.
- Identify several family and religious traditions.
- Describe why faith is important for families.
- Participate in a time of sharing and worship.

## Focus

These family enrichment workshops have been designed for one- or two-parent families. The focus is on strengthening relationships with family members.

With some minor adaptations, these workshops could also be used in "extended family" intergenerational groups.

## Session 1: Appreciating Each Other

*1. Get Acquainted (15–20 minutes)*

As people arrive, distribute copies of RM 15, "Wacky Words 1," for families to work on until the workshop begins.

When the group has assembled, welcome everyone. Tell participants that you hope this will be an enjoyable and growing experience.

Give each family unit a sheet of butcher paper and some crayons or felt-tip pens. Ask them to draw pictures of some of their family traditions (special holidays, the ways birthdays are celebrated, vacations, and so on). If families cannot think of any traditions, ask them to draw pictures of traditions they would like to begin.

Then have families share these pictures with each other. If your group has more than four or five families in it, divide into groups of three or four families for this process.

Tape the picture murals to the walls in your meeting room if possible.

Go over the answers for "Wacky Words 1":

*1a: 2 eggs over easy*
*1b: Cornerstone*
*1c: Down in the dumps*
*1d: Reading between the lines*
*2a: Ring around the rosy*
*2b: Six feet under ground*
*2c: Sleeping on the job*
*2d: Equal rights*
*3a: Split level*
*3b: Little house on the prairie*
*3c: Don't overreact*
*3d: Man in the moon*

*4a: Misunderstanding*
*4b: Check in the mail*
*4c: Count Dracula*
*4d: Pretty please with sugar on it*

## 2. Songs (5–10 minutes)

Use RM 16, "Family Fun Songs," to teach the group several fun songs. Mention what a good experience it can be for families to enjoy singing together. In order to help the group keep a common focus, you may want to wait until the last workshop to distribute copies of the song sheet for families to take home.

## 3. Input and Discussion (10–15 minutes)

Take a minute or two to introduce the themes for this series. If desired, distribute copies of RM 4, "Qualities of the Healthy Marriage and Family," to show some of the themes which will be used for these workshops.

Mention that one of the most important things we can do for the other family members is to express our appreciation and love to them.

Distribute copies of RM 17, "What the World Needs Now . . . ." Ask for volunteers to read each of the scripture verses provided on the worksheet. Ask participants to identify what each verse is challenging us to do.

Mention that God wants us not only to *express* our appreciation to other family members—to tell them what we appreciate and enjoy about them. God also wants us to learn to *receive* the appreciation of others—to be lovable as well as loving.

Briefly describe your own pilgrimage in learning to be a loving, appreciative, lovable person. Who helped you learn to be this way?

## 4. Small Group Discussion (10–15 minutes)

Divide into several small groups. If possible, ask that family members split into different groups, as a way of getting further acquainted with other participants.

Ask each group to make two lists:
- Reasons why some people find it hard to express appreciation and love to others, or receive it from them.
- Ways people can learn to be more loving and lovable.

### 5. Large Group Sharing (5–10 minutes)

Reassemble in the large group. Ask for a representative of each group to share their thoughts for each of these two areas. Develop a composite list on chalkboard or newsprint as participants share.

### 6. Family Sharing (10–15 minutes)

Ask that families sit in small circles in the room, with enough space between families so that privacy is ensured.

Ask that families do what is called an "affirmation bombardment" activity together. Have them give each family member a letter, beginning with A, then B, and so on.

Ask that the family group begin with person A. Other family members should share what they especially appreciate and enjoy about that person. Encourage participants to be as specific as possible.

Then person A responds by summarizing what was heard.

After person A is finished, the group moves on to person B and repeats the same process. The process continues until all family members have received the family's expressions of appreciation and love.

### 7. Wrap-Up (5–10 minutes)

Reassemble in the large group. Ask group members if they found it easier to give or receive these affirmations.

Summarize key points from this session about the importance of expressing and receiving appreciation and affirmation.

Conclude with a familiar Christian song, such as "God Is So Good." Then ask a participant to conclude with prayer, thanking God for this opportunity to be together and learn how to enjoy our families even more.

## Session 2: Spending Time Together

### 1. Get Acquainted (10–15 minutes)

As families arrive give them copies of RM 18, "Wacky Words 2," to work on until the entire group has arrived.

When the group has assembled, distribute sheets of butcher paper or newsprint and felt-tip pens or crayons to each family. Ask that the families draw pictures of what they enjoy doing together as a family.

Then have the families share their pictures with each other. In a large group, divide into groups of three or four families for this process. In a smaller group, the sharing can take place in one group.

Tape the pictures to the walls in your meeting room if possible.

Go over the answers for "Wacky Words 2":

*1a: Man overboard!*

*1b: Long underwear*

*1c: Upside down cake*

*1d: Crossroads*

*2a: Tricycle*

*2b: Trial separation*

*2c: Water under the bridge*

*2d: Life after death*

*3a: Paradise (pair of dice)*

*3b: Backwards glance*

*3c: Turn of the century*

*3d: Tooth decay*

*4a: Unfinished symphony*

*4b: What goes up must come down*

*4c: Three degrees below zero*

*4d: Growing pains*

## 2. Songs (5–10 minutes)

Enjoy several of the fun songs together. Ask families if they have other favorite songs they would like to teach the group.

## 3. Input and Discussion (10–15 minutes)

Summarize the theme of the last session—learning to enjoy sharing and receiving appreciation and love.

Mention that another important responsibility in being in a healthy family is to spend time together. Ask the group to identify several times that a family may be together. Ideas:

- Eating meals together
- Watching television
- Doing chores together

- Having fun together
- Riding to and from school.

As group members think of ideas, make a list on chalkboard or newsprint. Ask participants to tell how each of these times can help them enjoy each other more.

Reminisce for a moment about times you enjoyed with your own family as you were growing up.

### 4. Small Group Discussion (10–15 minutes)

Divide into several small groups. If possible, have family members separate into different groups as a means of getting acquainted with the others.

Ask groups to think of what makes it difficult for families to have enough quality time together. Acknowledge that some families may be together a lot—sitting in the same room, but not relating (such as with watching television).

### 5. Large Group Sharing (10–15 minutes)

Reassemble in the large group. Ask a volunteer from each group to share their thoughts. Make a composite list on chalkboard or newsprint as participants share. Ask which of the items are the most difficult to overcome. Put an asterisk (*) by those items.

Talk for a few moments about how to overcome some of these barriers to being together.

### 6. Family Sharing and Planning (10–15 minutes)

Ask that families sit again in small circles in the room, with enough space between families so that privacy is ensured.

Distribute copies of RM 19, "Family Togetherness," and RM 20, "A Family Contract." Guide families to begin by looking through the "Family Togetherness" worksheet and adding any of their own ideas to the list.

Then families are to use the "Family Contract" worksheet. Encourage them to fill in as many of the sections as are appropriate and possible to do. Then each family member should sign the contract and make a commitment to fulfill these promises in the next month, if at all possible.

*7. Wrap-Up (5–10 minutes)*

Reassemble in the large group. Ask group members to identify some of the activities they have promised to do.

Summarize the key points from this session about the importance of spending time together. In order to overcome some of the difficult barriers to doing this, a strong feeling of commitment and priority is needed.

Stand together in a large circle. Sing a familiar Christian song which group members suggest. Conclude with prayer. Ask that God will give each family the commitment that is needed to spend quality time together. Thank God for families.

## Session 3: Communicating Together

*1. Get Acquainted (10–15 minutes)*

As families arrive, give them copies of RM 21, "Wacky Words 3," to work on until the entire group has arrived.

When the group has assembled, point them to a large sheet of construction paper or newsprint on which you have lettered: "Communication is. . . ."

Ask group members to write words or draw pictures on the newsprint that completes the sentence. Mention that since this is like doing graffiti, they can draw the pictures or place their words any place on the paper that they want.

Take a minute or two to point out some of the key words and pictures.

Go over the answers for "Wacky Words 3":

*1a: Circles under the eyes*
*1b: Tiptoe through the tulips (tipped "toe")*
*1c: Safety in numbers*
*1d: Two-car garage*
*2a: See-through blouse*
*2b: Split-pea soup*
*2c: Turn over a new leaf*
*2d: Not up to par*
*3a: Jack-in-the-box*
*3b: Time flies*
*3c: Stick in the mud*

*3d: Raining cats and dogs*
*4a: Foot in the mouth*
*4b: Eyeball*
*4c: Walk on water*
*4d: A bird in the hand is worth more than two birds in the bush*

## 2. Songs (5–10 minutes)

Enjoy several of the fun songs together. Again, ask families if there are any other fun songs they would like to teach the group.

## 3. Input and Discussion (10–15 minutes)

Begin by mentioning how important communication is for healthy families. If people do not learn to share their thoughts and feelings, there is often conflict and confusion.

Say to the group: "If I tell you that I love you, but then I turn my back on you, how will you feel?"

"Or if I tell you I'm not angry but I sit glaring at you, what will you think?"

Distribute copies of RM 22, "Patterns of Communication." Briefly review and give an example of each pattern.

## 4. Discussion and Puppet Making (10–15 minutes)

Divide into two groups. If you have two leaders, one leader can take the children to another room, where they will make simple paper bag puppets for each family member. Use lunch-size paper bags. The children can draw faces on the puppets, so that when a person's arm and hand are inserted, they can make this "face" look like it is talking.

While the children are making the puppets, review the "Patterns" worksheet with the parents. Discuss why each of these patterns may be tempting to use at times. What are the limitations of each pattern? Why is leveling such a healthy style of communication? Deal with any questions the parents may have about communication in the family.

## 5. Family Role Play and Discussion (10–15 minutes)

Distribute copies of RM 23, "Family Situations." Ask each family to choose one of the situations which may sound like it may have happened to them. Briefly review the "Patterns" again.

Then ask each family member to choose one of the patterns of communication to try (do not tell the other family members what they will be doing). The first time, they should choose any of the patterns except leveling. Persons should use the puppets the children made for the role play.

After trying the situation for a few minutes, the families should stop and talk about what was difficult about each of the styles which was used. Which styles were the most frustrating? The easiest to use?

Then the families should try role playing the situation again, this time with all family members using the "leveling" pattern. After doing the role play, talk together about how this last role play was different from the others. What can be difficult about leveling? Yet why is it so important for healthy communication?

Encourage the families to talk about any changes in communication they would like to make.

### 6. Wrap-Up (5–10 minutes)

Reassemble in the large group. Deal with any questions or concerns the families may have about communication.

Mention again how vital communication is. It is so important that it tells a great deal about how healthy or unhealthy a family relationship really is.

Conclude with a song from the "Christian Songs for Families" worksheet (RM 23).

Ask one of the parents to conclude with prayer.

## Session 4: Sharing Our Faith

### 1. Get Acquainted (15–20 minutes)

As families arrive, give them copies of RM 25, "Brain Teasers," to work on while the others are arriving.

When the participants have assembled, divide into groups of two or three families each. Ask them to share some of the religious holidays or traditions which family members enjoy. Discuss what each of the religious holidays celebrates, and how family traditions help commemorate these occasions.

Reassemble in the large group. Go over the answers to the "Brain Teasers":

1. *Your date of birth plus your age*
2. *3 cows*
3. *4:05*
4. *10 crews*
5. *30 days*
6. *$20*
7. *8 half dollars; 80 pennies; 2 dimes*
8. *20 minutes*
9. *Over $21 million!*
10. *167*

## 2. Songs (10–15 minutes)

Enjoy a few of the fun songs together. Then sing one or two of the Christian songs as well. Families may have a favorite they would like to teach the group.

## 3. Input and Discussion (10–15 minutes)

Mention that one of the important ways that a family shows it is healthy is by sharing a faith together. This doesn't necessarily mean that all members of a family go to the same church or agree on every detail of religion. But it does mean that they see that their faith is important for everyday life.

Share how your faith has helped you personally, as well as in your family life.

Point out these key points regarding faith in the family (jot each idea on your chalkboard or newsprint as you share):

- Brings a sense of unity.
- Provides a framework for dealing with problems.
- Gives strength for dealing with problems.

Ask group members to identify other reasons why faith is important in their families.

## 4. Small Group Sharing and Discussion (10–15 minutes)

Divide into groups of two or three families each. Ask each group to make a list of important beliefs they have and how each is helpful in their families.

Acknowledge that this may be a difficult experience, since we don't always relate our faith specifically to our family life. But encourage them to come up with at least two or three ideas.

*5. Large Group Sharing (5–10 minutes)*

Reassemble in the large group. Ask a volunteer from each group to share the group's thoughts. Jot down their ideas on your chalkboard or newsprint. Clarify any points which may be vague.

*6. Concluding Worship (20–25 minutes)*

Conclude this family enrichment series with a time of informal sharing and worship. Here are some suggestions for this experience:

- *Songs.* Sing one or more of the Christian songs that the families enjoy.
- *Sharing.* Ask individuals to share how their faith has helped them personally and in their families.
- *Song.* Sing another of the Christian songs together.
- *Sharing.* Ask group members to share what has been meaningful or helpful to them in this series.
- *Poems.* Use the process described on RM 26, "Writing a Cinquain Poem." People can work alone, in pairs, or in families. Ask that several volunteers share their poems.
- *Next steps.* Tell the group how much you have enjoyed this series of workshops yourself, and how much you appreciate each person who has attended. Mention any workshop series that are planned for the immediate future. (See "Next Steps" for suggestions.) Distribute copies of RM 27, "Resources for Families."
- *The Lord's Prayer.* Say the prayer together.

## Next Steps

Consider offering at least one of the following series as a means for families to keep enriching their relationships:

- *Understanding Us* by Patrick Carnes—An excellent four session, 12-hour intergenerational workshop from the same people who produced the Couple Communication program. It does need leadership with some experience and expertise. An outstanding program. (See Family Enrichment, p. 89.)
- *Family Clusters*—An outstanding approach to enhancing family togetherness. Families who desire to keep meeting can use *Family Enrichment with Family Clusters,* as a resource in getting started. (See Family Enrichment, pp. 89–90.)

# PART FOUR

# ADDITIONAL RESOURCES

An asterisk (*) indicates a particular book is out of print. In this case, the book may be found at a library or resource center.

## Foundations

Adams, Bert N. *The Family: A Sociological Interpretation.* 3rd ed. Chicago: Rand McNally College Publishing Company, 1981. (Instructor's manual is available.)

Anthony, E. James, and Chiland, Colette, eds. *The Child in His Family: Children and Their Parents in a Changing World.* New York: John Wiley & Sons, 1978.*

Ardell, Donald. *High Level Wellness.* New York: Bantam Books, 1977.*

Axinn, Nancy; Hall, Olive A., and Paolucci, Beatrice. *Family Decision Making: An Ecosystem Approach.* New York: John Wiley & Sons, 1977.

Bane, Mary Jo. *Here To Stay: American Families in the 20th Century.* New York: Basic Books, Inc., 1978.

Beck, Dorothy Fahs. *Marriage and the Family under Challenge: An Outline of Issues, Trends, and Alternatives.* 2nd. ed. New York: Family Service Association of America, 1976. (Annotated bibliography by Emily Bradshaw.)

Berger, Brigitte, and Berger, Peter L. *War over the Family: Capturing the Middle Ground.* Garden City, N.Y.: Anchor/Doubleday, 1983.

Billingsley, Andrew. *Black Families in White America.* Englewood Cliffs, N.J.: Prentice-Hall, Inc., 1968.

Broderick, Carfred B. *Marriage and the Family.* Englewood Cliffs, N.J.: Prentice-Hall, Inc., 1979.

Corfman, Eunice, ed. *Families Today: A Research Sample on Families and Children*. 2 vols. Rockville, Md.: National Institute of Mental Health, 1979.*

Curran, Dolores. *Traits of a Healthy Family: Fifteen Traits Commonly Found in Healthy Families by Those Who Work with Them*. Minneapolis: Winston Press, 1984.

Davis, Glenn. *Childhood and History in America*. New York: Psycho-history Press, 1976. (Historical perspective on child-rearing modes from 1840 to 1965.)

Duvall, Evelyn M. *Marriage and Family Development*. 5th ed. Philadelphia: J.B. Lippincott Company, 1977.

Fisher, Seymour, and Fisher, Rhoda L. *What We Really Know about Child Rearing*. New York: Basic Books, 1976.*

The General Mills American Family Report 1978-79. *Family Health in an Era of Stress*. Minneapolis: General Mills, 1979.*

Glazer-Malbin, Nona, ed. *Old Family/New Family: Interpersonal Relationships*. New York: D. Van Nostrand Company, 1975. (Research-oriented articles on marriage and family.)*

Greeley, Andrew, ed. *The Family in Crisis or in Transition*. New York: The Seabury Press, 1979.

Gross, Beatrice, and Gross, Ronald, eds. *The Children's Rights Movement: Overcoming the Oppression of Young People*. Garden City, N.Y.: Anchor Press/Doubleday, 1977.*

Helfer, Ray E., and Kempe, C. Henry. *Child Abuse and Neglect: The Family and the Community*. Cambridge, Mass.: Ballinger Publishing Company, 1976. (Helpful information on family dysfunctions, family therapy, and community programs.)

Justice, Rita, and Justice, Blaire. *The Abusing Family*. New York: Human Sciences Press, 1976. (Child abuse: description, causes, preventative measures.)

Kantor, David, and Lehr, William. *Inside the Family: Toward a Theory of Family Process*. New York: Harper Colophone Books, 1975.

Keniston, Kenneth, and the Carnegie Council on Children. *All Our Children*. New York: Harcourt Brace Jovanovich, 1978.

Klein, Donald C., and Goldson, Stephen E., eds. *Primary Prevention: An Idea Whose Time Has Come*. Rockville, Md.: National Institute of Mental Health, 1977.*

Knox, David H. *Exploring Marriage and the Family*. Glenview, Ill.: Scott, Foresman and Company, 1979.

Lewis, J. M.; Phillips, Virginia Austin; Beaver, Robert; and Gossett, John T. *No Single Thread: Psychological Health in Family Systems.* New York: Brunner/Mazel, Publishers, 1976. (Long term pioneering study on how healthy families function, focusing especially on interactional variables.)

Leichter, Hope, ed. *Families and Communities As Educators.* New York: Teachers College Press, 1979.

Martinez, J. L., and Mendoza, Richard H. ed. *Chicano Psychology.* 2nd ed. New York: Academic Press, 1984.

Masnick, George, and Bane, Mary Jo. *The Nation's Families: 1960-1990.* Boston: Auburn House Publishing Co., 1980.

Mindel, Charles H., and Habenstein, Robert W., eds. *Ethnic Families in America.* 2nd ed. New York: Elsevier, 1981.

Moore, Joan W. *Mexican Americans.* 2nd ed. Englewood Cliffs, N.J.: Prentice-Hall, Inc., 1976.

Murstein, Bernard I. *Love, Sex, and Marriage Through the Ages.* New York: Springer Publishing Company, 1974.

National Research Council. *Toward a National Policy for Children and Families.* Washington, D.C.: National Academy of Sciences, 1976. (Overview of the state of American families and children and related issues. Lists approaches to family services.)

Olson, David H., and Hamilton I. McCubbin & Associates. *Families: What Makes Them Work.* Beverly Hills, Calif.: Sage Publications, Inc., 1983.

Patterson, Gerald R. *Families: Application of Social Learning to Family Life.* Revised. Champaign, Ill.: Research Press, 1975. (Revised edition.)

Pinkney, Alphonso. *Black Families.* 2nd ed. Englewood Cliffs, N.J.: Prentice-Hall, Inc., 1975.*

Rapoport, Rhona; Rapoport, Robert N.; Sirelit, Ziona and Keus, Stephen. *Fathers, Mothers, and Society: Perspectives on Parenting.* New York: Vintage Books, 1980.

Rice, Robert M. *American Family Policy: Content and Context.* New York: Family Service Association of America, 1977.*

Richards, Lawrence O. *A Theology of Christian Education.* Grand Rapids, Mich.: Zondervan Publishing House, 1975.

Richards, Martin P.M., ed. *The Integration of a Child into a Social World.* London: Cambridge University Press, 1974.*

Scanzoni, John. "Reconsidering Family Policy: Status Quo or a Force for Change?" *Journal of Family Issues* Vol. 3, No. 3, (September 1982): 277-95.

_____ . *Shaping Tomorrow's Family: Theory and Policy for the 21st Century.* Beverly Hills, Calif.: Sage Publications, Inc., 1983.

Scanzoni, Letha, and Scanzoni, John. *Men, Women and Change: A Sociology of Marriage and Family.* 2nd ed. New York: McGraw-Hill Book Company, 1981.

Schulz, David A., and Rodgers, Stanley F. *Marriage, the Family, and Personal Fulfillment.* 3rd ed. Englewood Cliffs, N.J.: Prentice-Hall, Inc., 1985. (Text edition.)

Senn, Milton J. *Speaking Out for America's Children.* New Haven, Conn.: Yale University Press, 1977.

Sheek, G. William. *A Nation for Families: Family Life Education in Public Schools.* Washington D.C.: American Home Economics Association, 1984.*

Skolnick, Arlene, and Skolnick, Jerome. *Family in Transition.* 4th ed. Boston: Little, Brown and Company, 1983.

Stack, Carol B. *All Our Kin: Strategies for Survival in a Black Community.* New York: Harper & Row, Publishers, 1975.

Stinnett, Nick; Chesser, Barbara; and Defrain, John, eds. *Building Family Strengths: Blueprints for Action.* Lincoln, Neb.: University of Nebraska Press, 1979.*

Stinnett, Nick; Chesser, Barbara; and DeFrain, John, eds. *Family Strengths: Positive Models for Family Life.* Lincoln, Neb.: University of Nebraska Press, 1980.

Toman, Walter. *Family Constellation* 3rd ed. New York: Springer Publishing Company, 1976.

*Wellness Perspectives: Journal of Individual, Family, and Community Wellness.* Lincoln, Neb.: Wellness Perspectives, University of Nebraska.

Westerhoff, John H. "The Church and the Family." *Religious Education,* Spring 1983.

Williams, Gertrude J., and Money, John, eds. *Traumatic Abuse and Neglect of Children at Home.* Baltimore: Johns Hopkins University Press, 1980.

## Implementation

*Being God's Family: A Notebook for Ministry.* Office of Social Welfare, The Episcopal Church Center, 815 Second Ave., New York, NY 10017.

Benson, Jeanette, and Hilyard, Jack. *Becoming Family.* Winona, Minn.: St. Mary's College Press, 1978.

Brown, Raymond K. *Reach Out to Singles: A Challenge to Ministry.* Philadelphia: Westminster, 1979.

"The Church and Families." Melbourne, Australia: Globe Press, 1982. (Available from: The Joint Board of Christian Education, 177 Collins St., Melbourne, Victoria 3000, Australia.)

Clinebell, Howard. *Growth Groups.* Nashville: Abingdon, 1977.*

Coleman, Lyman. *Serendipity* Books. Waco, Tex.: Word. (A helpful series for relational studies—for leadership, couples, parents, and families. Those which are particularly written for use with family groupings are: *Destiny,* Discovering Your Call; *Come Fly,* Discovering a New Lifestyle; and *Hassle,* Dealing with Family Relationships.)

"A Compilation of Protestant Denomination Statements on Families and Sexuality." (Available from the Commission on Family Ministries and Human Sexuality, National Council of Churches, 475 Riverside Dr., Seventh Floor, New York, New York 10115.)

"A Directory of Resources on Family Ministries and Human Sexuality." (Produced by eight denominations. Available from the Commission on Family Ministries and Human Sexuality, National Council of Churches, 475 Riverside Dr., Seventh Floor, New York, N.Y. 10115.)

*The Family Album: Resource for Family Life Ministry.* (Produced by United Church of Christ, Board for Homeland Ministries. Available from Church Leadership Resources, 1400 North 7th St., St. Louis, Mo. 63106. Telephone 800-325-7061.)

*Family Life Ministry Notebook.* The Office of Family Life, General Program Council, Reformed Church in America. (Box 803, Orange City, Iowa 51041.)

*Family Ministry: Resource and Program Guide.* (Developed by the Family Ministry Team, Presbyterian Church USA. Available from Materials Distribution Service, 421 Ponce de Leon Ave., Atlanta, Ga. 30365. Telephone 404-873-1549.)

Guernsey, Dennis B. *A New Design for Family Ministry.* Elgin, Ill.: David C. Cook, 1982.

Larson, Jim. *Family Ministry Models for the 80's.* Chicago: Department of Christian Education, The Evangelical Covenant Church, 1980.

Larson, Jim, and Larson, Jill. *Celebrating Togetherness.* Chicago: Department of Christian Education, The Evangelical Covenant Church, 1973.

Leonard, Joe. *Planning for Family Ministry: A Guide for the Teaching Church.* Valley Forge, Pa.: Judson Press, 1982.

Lindner, Eileen W. et. al. *When Churches Mind the Children: A Study of Day Care in Local Parishes.* Ypsilanti, Mich.: High/Scope Press, 1983. (A workbook titled *Helping Churches Mind the Children: A Guide for Church-Housed Child Day Care Programs* is also available.)

Louthan, Sheldon, and Martin, Grant. *Family Ministries in Your Church.* Ventura, Calif.: Regal Books, 1977.*

Mace, David, and Mace, Vera. *Marriage Enrichment in the Church.* Nashville: Broadman, 1977.

National Institute of Mental Health. *Parents Are People, Too.* Washington, D.C.: U.S. Department of Health, Education, and Welfare, 1975. (Revised edition. Description of family life education programs, communication workshops, helpful organizations for enrichment of family life.)*

Otto, Herbert A., ed. *Marriage and Family Enrichment: New Perspectives and Programs.* Nashville: Abingdon, 1976.

Sell, Charles. *Family Ministry: Family Life through the Church.* Grand Rapids, Mich.: Zondervan, 1981.

Williamson, David. *Group Power: How to Develop, Lead and Help Groups Achieve Goals.* Englewood Cliffs, N.J.: Prentice-Hall, Inc., 1982.

# Marriage Enrichment

## Preparation for Marriage

*Building a Christian Marriage: Premarriage Counseling Resource.* St. Louis: Concordia, 1984. (Video based.)

Dinkmeyer, Don et al. *Preparation for Effective Family Living.* Circle Pines, Minn.: Guidance Service, 1985. (A complete instructional program for young adults.)

Oates, Wayne E., and Rowatt, Wade. *Before You Marry Them: A Premarital Guidebook for Pastors.* Nashville: Broadman, 1975.*

Rock, Stanley A. *This Time Together: A Guide for Premarital Counseling.* Grand Rapids, Mich.: Zondervan, 1980.*

Smith, Antoinette, and Smith, Leon. *Growing Love in Christian Marriage.* Nashville: The United Methodist Publishing House, 1981. (A Couple's Manual is also available for this premarital series.)*

## Marriage Enrichment

*Building a Christian Marriage: Marriage Enrichment Resource.* St. Louis: Concordia, 1984. (Video based.)

Coleman, Lyman, and Gallagher, Chuck. *Evenings for Couples*. New York: William H. Sadlier, 1976. (Includes a Leader's Guide, Response Sheets and a book for couples to read.)\*

Dinkmeyer, Don, and Carlson, Jon. *Training in Marriage Enrichment*. Circle Pines, Minn.: American Guidance Service, 1985. (A 10-session training program for people who work with couples.)

Miller, Sherod; Nunnally, Elman; and Wackman, Daniel. *Couple Communication: A Marriage Enrichment Program*. Minneapolis: Interpersonal Communication Programs, Inc. (An excellent 4-session communication program which is helpful to engaged and married couples alike.)

Penner, Clifford, and Penner, Joyce. *Sexual Fulfillment in Marriage*. Wheaton, Ill.: Family Concern, 1977. (A multimedia kit.)

Potts, Nancy. *Beginning Again: The Challenge of the Formerly Married*. Elgin, Ill.: David C. Cook, 1977. (A multimedia kit on divorce, singleness and new beginnings.)

Vander Haar, Trudy, and Vander Haar, Del. *Growing in Marriage*. Philadelphia: Geneva Press, 1984. (Includes both a Leader's Guide and Worksheets.)\*

Wright, H. Norman. *Pillars of Marriage*. Ventura, Calif.: Regal Books, 1979. (A Leader's Guide is also available.)

# Resources for Couples

## Sexuality/Sex Roles

Barback, Lonnie. *For Yourself: The Fulfillment of Female Sexuality*. Garden City, N.Y.: Anchor Press/Doubleday, 1975.

Brannon, Robert, and David, Deborah S., eds. *The Forty-Nine Percent Majority: The Male Sex Role*. Menlo Park, Calif.: Addison-Wesley Publishing Company, 1976.

Chipouras, Sophia; Cornelius, Debra; Daniels, Susan M.; and Makas, Elaine. *Who Cares? A Handbook on Sex Education and Counseling Services for Disabled People*. Washington, D.C.: George Washington University, 1979.\*

Clinebell, Charlotte Holt. *Counseling for Liberation*. Philadelphia: Fortress Press, 1976.

Dowling, Colette. *The Cinderella Complex: Women's Hidden Fear of Independence*. New York: Summit Books, 1981.

Friday, Nancy. *My Mother, My Self.* New York: Dell Publishing Co., Inc., 1981.

Frieze, Irene; Parsons, Jacquelynne; Johnson, Paula; Ruble, Diane; and Zellman, Gail. *Women and Sex Roles: Social Psychological Perspective.* New York: W. W. Norton and Company, 1978. (Instructor's manual available.)

Jewett, Paul K. *Man as Male and Female.* Grand Rapids, Mich.: Eerdmans, 1975.*

Katchadourian, Herant A., and Lunde, Donald T. *Fundamentals of Human Sexuality.* 3rd ed. New York: Holt, Rinehart, and Winston, Inc., 1980.

Hite, Shere. *The Hite Report: A Nationwide Study of Female Sexuality.* New York: Dell Publishing Co., 1976.*

Lipman-Blumen, Jean. *Gender Roles and Power.* Englewood Cliffs, N.J.: Prentice-Hall, 1984.

McGuinan, Dorothy, ed. *Women's Lives: New Theory, Research & Policy.* Ann Arbor, Mich.: The University of Michigan Center for Continuing Education of Women, 1980.*

Nelson, James B. *Embodiment.* Minneapolis: Augsburg, 1979.

Nowinski, Joseph. *Becoming Satisfied: A Man's Guide to Sexual Fulfillment.* Englewood Cliffs, N.J.: Prentice-Hall, 1980.

Olson, Richard P. *Changing Male Roles in Today's World: A Christian Perspective for Men and the Women Who Care about Them.* Valley Forge, Pa.: Judson Press, 1982.

O'Reilly, Jane. *The Girl I Left Behind: The Housewife's Moment of Truth and Other Feminist Ravings.* New York: Macmillan Publishing Co., Inc., 1984.

Penner, Clifford, and Penner, Joyce. *The Gift of Sex: A Christian Guide to Sexual Fulfillment.* Waco, Tex.: Word Books, 1981.

Rich, Adrienne. *Of Woman Born: Motherhood As Experience and Institution.* New York: Bantam Books, 1976.

Sangiuliano, Iris. *In Her Time.* New York: Morrow Quill Paperbacks, 1978.

Sargent, Alice G. *Beyond Sex Roles* 2nd ed. St. Paul: West Publishing Co., 1985.

Scanzoni, Letha, and Hardesty, Nancy. *All We're Meant to Be: A Biblical Approach to Women's Liberation.* Waco, Tex.: Word Books, Publisher, 1974.*

Small, Dwight Hervey. *Christian, Celebrate Your Sexuality.* Old Tappan, N.J.: Fleming H. Revell, 1974.*

Smedes, Lewis B. *Sex for Christians*. Grand Rapids, Mich.: Eerdmans, 1976.

Wilson, Sam, et. al. *Human Sexuality: A Text with Readings*. St. Paul: West Publishing Co., 1977. (Instructor's manual available.)

## Marriage

Ahlem, Lloyd. *Living with Stress*. 2nd ed. Ventura, Calif.: Regal Books, 1982.

Ashley, P. P. *Oh Promise Me, But Put It in Writing: Living Together Agreements Without, Before, During, and After Marriage*. New York: McGraw-Hill Book Company, 1980.

Augsburger, David. *Caring Enough to Confront*. Ventura, Calif.: Regal Books, 1980. (Revised edition. Guidelines for handling conflict and anger in marriage and family.)

_____ . *When Enough Is Enough*. Ventura, Calif.: Regal Books, 1984.

Balswick, Jack. *Why I Can't Say I Love You*. Waco, Tex.: Word Books, 1978.*

Bright, Richard, and Stapleton, Jean. *Equal Marriage*. Nashville: Abingdon, 1976.*

Chartier, Jan, and Chartier, Myron. *Trusting Together in God*. St. Meinrad, Ind.: Abbey, 1984.

Demarest, Gary. *Christian Alternatives Within Marriage*. Waco, Tex.: Word Books, 1978.*

Drakeford, John W. *Marriage: How to Keep a Good Thing Growing*. Nashville: Impact Books, 1979.*

Freudenberger, Herbert. *Burn Out: How to Beat the High Cost of Success*. New York: Bantam Books, 1980.*

Gould, Roger. *Transformations: Growth and Change in Adult Life*. New York: Simon and Schuster, 1979.

Halpern, Howard. *Cutting Loose: An Adult Guide to Coming to Terms with Your Parents*. New York: Bantam Books, 1976.*

Hunt, Joan, and Hunt, Richard. *Growing Love in Christian Marriage: Couple's Manual*. Nashville: The United Methodist Publishing House, 1981.

Katz, Sanford N., and Inker, Monrie L. *Fathers, Husbands and Lovers: Legal Rights and Responsibilities*. Chicago: American Bar Association, 1979.

Lederer, William J., and Jackson, Don D. *The Mirages of Marriage.* New York: W. W. Norton & Company, Inc., 1968. (Deals with false assumptions of modern marriage, and how to make marriage work.)

Levinson, Daniel. *The Seasons of a Man's Life.* New York: Alfred A. Knopf, 1978.

McCrary, James Leslie. *Freedom and Growth in Marriage.* Santa Barbara, Calif.: Hamilton Publishing Company, 1975.*

Mace, David R. *Success in Marriage.* Nashville: Abingdon, 1980.

Mace, David, and Mace, Vera. *How to Have a Happy Marriage.* Nashville: Abingdon, 1983.

———. *We Can Have Better Marriages If We Really Want Them.* Nashville: Abingdon, 1974. (Valuable overview of marriage today, as well as resources for marriage enrichment.)

Marcus, Genevieve G., and Smith, Robert Lee. *Equal Time: Maintaining a Balance in Today's Intimate Relationships.* New York: Frederick Fell Publishers, 1982.

Miller, Sherod; Nunnally, Elam W.; and Wackman, Daniel B. *Couple Communication 1: Talking Together.* Minneapolis: Interpersonal Communication Programs, 1979.

O'Neill, Nena, and O'Neill, George. *Shifting Gears.* New York: Avon Books, 1975.

Paul, Jordan, and Paul, Margaret. *Do I Have to Give Up Me to Be Loved by You?* Minneapolis: Comp Care, 1983.

Powell, John. *The Secret of Staying in Love.* Niles, Ill.: Argus Communications, 1974.

———. *Why Am I Afraid to Love?* Niles, Ill.: Argus Communications, 1972. (Revised edition.)

———. *Why Am I Afraid to Tell You Who I Am?* Niles, Ill.: Argus Communications, 1969.

Rogers, Carl R. *Becoming Partners: Marriage and Its Alternatives.* New York: Dell Publishing Company, 1973.

Rubin, Lillian. *Intimate Strangers: Men and Women Together.* New York: Harper & Row, Publishers, 1983.

Schwartz, Roslyn, and Schwartz, Leonard J. *Becoming a Couple: Making the Most of Every Stage of Your Relationship.* Englewood Cliffs, N.J.: Prentice-Hall, 1980.

Shedd, Charlie W. *Talk To Me!* Garden City, N.Y.: Doubleday & Company, Inc., 1983. (Revised and expanded edition. Guidelines for women to help their husbands communicate. Helpful for husbands, too.)

Sheehy, Gail. *Passages: Predictable Crises of Adult Life*. New York: Bantam Books, 1976.

_____ . *Pathfinders*. New York: Bantam Books, 1981.

Strayhorn, Joseph M., Jr. *Talking It Out: A Guide to Effective Communication and Problem Solving*. Champaign, Ill.: Research Press Company, 1977.

Suid, Roberta; Bradley, Buff; Suid, Murray; and Eastman, Jean. *Married, Etc.: A Sourcebook for Couples*. Menlo Park, Calif.: Addison-Wesley Publishing Company, 1976. (Catalog format. Resources for couples.)*

Tournier, Paul. *To Understand Each Other*. Richmond, Va.: John Knox Press, 1967. (A classic treatment of intimacy and harmony in marriage.)

Tubesing, Donald. *Kicking Your Stress Habits: A Do-It-Yourself Guide for Coping with Stress*. New York: A Signet Book/New American Library, 1981.

## Divorce/Remarriage/Stepparenting

Adam, John H., and Adam, Nancy. *Divorce: How and When to Let Go*. Englewood Cliffs, N.J.: Prentice-Hall, 1979.

Block, Joel D. *To Marry Again: The Other Man—The Other Woman*. New York: Gross & Dunlap, 1979.*

Berman, Claire. *Making It as a Stepparent: New Roles, New Rules*. Garden City, N.Y.: Doubleday and Co., 1980.*

Correu, Larry M. *Beyond the Broken Marriage*. Philadelphia: The Westminster Press, 1982.

Duberman, Lucille. *The Reconstituted Family: A Study of Remarried Couples and Their Children*. Chicago: Nelson-Hall Publishers, 1975.

Duncan, T. Roger, and Duncan, Darlene. *You're Divorced, But Your Children Aren't*. Englewood Cliffs, N.J.: Prentice-Hall, 1979.

Gardner, Richard. *The Parents' Book About Divorce*. Garden City, N.Y.: Doubleday & Company, 1979.

Jacobson, Doris S. "Stepfamilies: Myths and Realities." *Social Work* (May 1979): 202-207.

Jones, Shirley Maxwell. "Divorce and Remarriage: A New Beginning, A New Set of Problems." *Journal of Divorce* 2 (Winter 1978): 217–26.

Kalter, Suzy. *Instant Parent: A Guide for Stepparents, Part-Time Parents, and Grandparents*. New York: A and W Publishers, 1979.*

Levinger, George, and Moles, Oliver C. *Divorce and Separation*. New York: Basic Books, 1979.

Monkrers, Peter R. *Ministry with the Divorced.* New York: Pilgrim Press, 1985.

Reed, Bobbie. *Stepfamilies: Living in Christian Harmony.* St. Louis, Mo.: Concordia Publishing House, 1980.*

Small, Dwight Hervey. *The Right to Remarry.* Old Tappan, N.J.: Fleming H. Revell Company, 1975.*

Smoke, Jim. *Growing Through Divorce.* Irvine, Calif.: Harvest House Publishers, 1979.

_____ . *Suddenly Single.* Old Tappan, N.J.: Fleming H. Revell Company, 1982.

Visher, Emily B., and Visher, John. *Stepfamilies: A Guide to Working with Stepparents and Stepchildren.* New York: Brunn/Mazel, 1980.

Wallerstein, Judith, and Kelly, Joan. *Surviving the Breakup: How Children and Parents Cope with Divorce.* New York: Basic Books, 1980.

Westoff, Leslie Aldridge. *The Second Time Around: Remarriage in America.* New York: The Viking Press, 1977.*

Women in Transition, Inc. *Women in Transition: A Feminist Handbook on Separation and Divorce.* New York: Charles Scribner's Sons, 1975.

## Parent Education

Darcy-Berube, Francoise, and Berube, John Paul. *To Be a Parent: A Christian Renewal Program for Parents of Young Children.* New York: Paulist Press, 1973. (A Catholic-oriented program for parent education. Creative, stimulating.)*

Dinkmeyer, Don, and McKay, Gary D. *Systematic Training for Effective Parenting.* Circle Pines, Minn.: American Guidance Service, Inc., 1976. (A 9-session parent study group resource, including Parent's Book and Leader's Guide.)

Dinkmeyer, Don, and McKay, Gary D. *The Parent's Guide: Systematic Training for Effective Parenting of Teens.* Circle Pines, Minn.: American Guidance Service, 1984. (Complete resources for parent education are available.)

Gallagher, Chuck. *Parents Are Lovers.* New York: William H. Sadlier, 1976. (A Leader's Guide and Response Sheets are also available and provide four studies for parents.)

Larson, Jim. *Teaching Christian Values in the Family: A Guide for Parents.* Elgin, Ill.: David C. Cook, 1982. (A multimedia kit which provides 13 sessions for parents.)

Popkin, Michael H. *Active Parenting*. Atlanta, Ga. (2996 Grandview Ave., Suite 312, Atlanta, Ga. 30305; telephone: 1 800-241-1667 or 404-231-2172. A parent education program which includes videotapes, Leader's Guide and Parent's Handbook.)

Wagonseller, Bill R., et. al. *The Art of Parenting*. Champaign, Ill.: Research Press, 1977. (A five-session parenting workshop, including five filmstrips and cassettes, Leader's Guide, and Parent's Workbook Review Manuals.)

Wakefield, Norman. *Building Self-Esteem in the Family*. Elgin, Ill.: David C. Cook, 1977. (A multimedia kit.)

White, E. E. *The Art of Nurturing: On-the-Job Training for Parents and Teachers in Adult/Child Relationships*. Palo Alto, Calif.: Peek Publications, 1977.*

Y.M.C.A. *Family Enrichment: A Group Learning Experience for Parents of Elementary Children*. New York: Association Press, 1976. (Three separate projects for family enrichment—for fathers, mothers, or couples. Includes Leader's Manual, Parent's Manual, and cassette.)*

# Resources for Parents

## Parenting

Babcock, Dorothy E., and Keepers, Terry D. *Raising Kids OK*. New York: Avon, 1977.

Bell, Ruth, and Wildflower, Leni. *Talking with Your Teenagers: A Book for Parents*. New York: Random House, 1984.

Benson, Dennis C., and Stewart, Stan J. *The Ministry of the Child*. Nashville: Abingdon, 1979.

Bittman, Sam, and Zalk, Sue. *Expectant Fathers*. New York: Hawthorne Books, 1979.

Bottel, Helen. *Parents' Survival Kit: A Reassuring Guide to Living Through Your Child's Teen-age Years*. Garden City, N.Y.: Doubleday, 1979.*

Bloomfield, Harold. *Making Peace with Your Parents*. New York: Ballantine Books, 1983.

Briggs, Dorothy Corkille. *Celebrate Your Self: Making Life Work for You*. Garden City, N.Y.: Doubleday, 1977.

_____ . *Your Child's Self-Esteem: The Key to His Life*. Garden City, N.Y.: Doubleday, 1970.

Buth, Lenore. *Sexuality: God's Precious Gift to Parents and Children.* St. Louis: Concordia, 1983.

Calderone, Mary, and Johnson, Eric. *The Family Book About Sexuality.* New York: Harper and Row, 1981.

Calderone, Mary, and Ramey, James. *Talking with Your Child About Sex: Questions and Answers for Children from Birth to Puberty.* New York: Random House, 1983.

Calladine, Carole, and Calladine, Andrew. *Raising Siblings.* New York: Delacorte Press, 1979.

Caplan, Frank, ed. *Parents' Yellow Pages,* Garden City, N.Y.: Anchor Press/Doubleday, 1978.*

Christian Parent Series. St. Louis: Concordia. (12 titles covering the family life cycle.)

Clark, Jean Illsley. *Self-Esteem: A Family Affair.* Minneapolis: Winston Press, 1978.*

Dodson, Fitzhugh. *How to Father.* New York: New American Library, 1975.

Dreikurs, Rudolph, and Stolz, Vicki. *Children: The Challenge.* New York: Hawthorne, 1964.

Dreikurs, Rudolph, and Grey, Loren. *Logical Consequences: A New Approach to Discipline.* New York: Hawthorne, 1968.

Faber, Adele, and Mazlish, Elaine. *Liberated Parents—Liberated Children.* New York: Avon, 1974.

Fournier, Barbara, and Fournier, George. *Pre-Parenting: A Guide for Planning Ahead.* Englewood Cliffs, N.J.: Prentice-Hall, 1980.

Fraiberg, Selma H. *The Magic Years: Understanding and Handling the Problems of Early Childhood.* New York: Charles Scribner's Sons, 1959.*

Gilbert, Sara D. *What's a Father For?* New York: Warner, 1975.*

Ginott, Haim G. *Between Parent and Child.* New York: Avon, 1965.

_____ . *Between Parent and Teenager.* New York: Avon, 1969.

Gordon, Sol, and Gordon, Judith. *Raising a Child Conservatively in a Sexually Permissive World.* New York: Simon & Schuster, 1983.

Gordon, Thomas. *Parent Effectiveness Training: The Tested New Way to Raise Responsible Children.* New York: Peter H. Wyden, 1970.

Gow, Kathleen. *Yes, Virginia, There Is Right and Wrong.* New York: John Wiley and Sons, 1980.

Graubard, Paul S. *Positive Parenthood.* Indianapolis: Bobbs-Merrill, 1977.

Hale, Nathan Cabot. *Birth of a Family: The New Role of the Father in Childbirth.* Garden City, N.Y.: Anchor Press/Doubleday, 1979.*

Hathaway, Marjie, and Hathaway, Jay. *Children at Birth.* Sherman Oaks, Calif.: Academy Publishers, 1978.

Haystead, Wes. *Teaching Your Child About God.* Ventura, Calif.: Regal Books, 1983.

Hersh, Richard; Paolitto, Diana; and Reimer, Joseph. *Promoting Moral Growth: From Piaget to Kohlberg.* New York: Longman, 1979.*

Holman, William E. *Child Sense.* New York: Basic Books, 1977.

Howell, Mary. *Helping Ourselves: Families and the Human Network.* Boston: Beacon Press, 1975.*

James, Muriel. *Transactional Analysis for Moms and Dads.* Menlo Park, Calif.: Addison-Wesley, 1974.*

Johnson, Spencer. *The One Minute Father.* New York: William Morrow, 1983.

——————— . *The One Minute Mother.* New York: William Morrow, 1983.

Ketterman, Grace, and Ketterman, Herbert L. *The Complete Book of Baby and Child Care.* Old Tappan, N.J.: Fleming H. Revell, 1981. (Revised and updated.)

Klein, Carole. *How It Feels to Be a Child.* New York: Harper, 1975.*

Larson, Jim. *Growing a Healthy Family.* Minneapolis: Augsburg Publishing House, 1986.

——————— . *Rights, Wrongs, and In-Betweens: Guiding Our Children to Christian Maturity.* Minneapolis: Augsburg, 1984.

Lerman, Saf. *Parent Awareness: Positive Parenting for the 1980s.* Minneapolis: Winston, 1981.

——————— . *Responsive Parenting.* Circle Pines, Minn.: American Guidance Service, 1984.*

Lewis, Jerry M. *How's Your Family? A Guide to Identifying Your Family's Strengths and Weaknesses.* New York: Brunner/Maxel, 1979.

Lynn, David B. *The Father: His Role in Child Development.* Monterey, Calif.: Brooks/Cole, 1974.*

Mayle, Peter. *How to Be a Pregnant Father.* Secaucus, N.J.: Lyle Stuart, 1977.

McDermott, John. *Raising Cain (& Abel, Too): The Parent's Book of Sibling Rivalry.* New York: Wyden Books, 1980.*

McDiarmid, Norma J., et. al. *Loving and Learning: Interacting with Your Child from Birth to Three.* New York: Harcourt Brace Jovanovich, 1977.

McGinnis, Kathleen, and McGinnis, James. *Parenting for Peace and Justice.* Maryknoll, N.Y.: Orbis Books, 1981.

Meier, Paul D. *Christian Child-Rearing and Personality Development.* Grand Rapids, Mich.: Baker, 1977.

Miller, Mary Susan. *Child-Stress! Understanding and Answering Stress Signals of Infants, Children, and Teenagers.* Garden City, N.Y.: Doubleday, 1982.*

Munnion, Catherine, and Grender, Iris. *The Open House: Learning Made Easy for Parents and Children.* New York: St. Martin's Press, 1976.*

Narramore, Bruce. *Parenting with Love and Limits.* Grand Rapids, Mich.: Zondervan, 1982.

Naylor, Phyllis Reynolds. *Getting Along in Your Family.* Nashville: Abingdon, 1976.

Oates, Wayne, ed. Christian Care Books. Philadelphia: Westminster Press. (Books include a wide variety of family issues.)

Oraker, James, and Meredith, Char. *Almost Grown: A Christian Guide for Parents of Teenagers.* San Francisco: Harper and Row, 1980.

Otto, Herbert A. *The New Sex Education.* Chicago: Follett, 1978.

Pedersen, J. Allan, ed. *For Families Only: Answering the Tough Questions Parents Ask.* Wheaton, Ill.: Tyndale, 1977.*

Pringle, Mia Kellmer. *The Needs of Children.* New York: Schocken, 1975.*

Reynolds, William. *The American Father.* New York: Pocket Books, 1978.

Rogers, Fred, and Head, Barry. *Mister Rogers Talks with Parents.* New York: Berkley Books, 1983.

Satir, Virginia. *Peoplemaking.* Palo Alto, Calif.: Science and Behavior Books, 1972.

Scanzoni, Letha. *Sex Is a Parent Affair.* 2nd ed. New York: Bantam, 1982.*

Schaeffer, Edith. *What Is a Family?* Old Tappan, N.J.: Fleming H. Revell, 1975.

Scharf, Peter; McCoy, William; and Ross, Diane. *Growing Up Moral.* Minneapolis: Winston, 1979.*

Seamands, David A. *Problem Solving in the Christian Family.* Carol Stream, Ill.: Creation House, 1975.*

Shedd, Charlie. *The Best Dad Is a Good Lover.* Kansas City: Sheed Andrews and McMeel, 1977.

Shedd, Charlie W. *You Can Be a Great Parent,* Waco, Tex.: Word, 1970.

Sheffield, Margaret, and Bewley, Sheila. *Where Do Babies Come From?* New York: Alfred A. Knopf, 1973.

Simon, Sidney B., and Olds, Sally W. *Helping Your Child Learn Right from Wrong.* New York: Simon and Schuster, 1977.

Stein, Edward V. *Fathering—Fact or Fable?* Nashville: Abingdon, 1977.

Steinberg, David. *Father Journal: Five Years of Awakening to Fatherhood.* New York: Times Change Press, 1977.

Stonehouse, Catherine. *Patterns in Moral Development.* Waco, Tex.: Word, 1980.*

Stoop, Dave, and Stoop, Jan. *The Total(ed) Parent: Hope for Parents Caught in the Struggle.* Irvine, Calif.: Harvest House, 1978.*

Sullivan, S. Adams. *The Father's Almanac.* Garden City, N.Y.: Doubleday, 1980.

Swihart, Judson. *How to Treat Your Family as Well as You Treat Your Friends.* Ventura, Cal.: Regal Books, 1982.

Uslander, Arlene S.; Weiss, Caroline; and Telman, Judith. *Sex Education for Today's Child.* New York: Association Press, 1977.*

Ward, Ted. *Values Begin at Home.* Wheaton, Ill.: Victor, 1979.

Weinberg, Richard, and Weinberg, Lynn. *Parent Prerogatives: How to Handle Teacher Misbehavior and Other School Disorders.* Chicago: Nelson-Hall, 1979.

Westerhoff, John H. *Bringing Up Children in the Christian Faith.* Minneapolis: Winston Press, 1980.

Whelan, Elizabeth M. *A Baby? . . . Maybe: Making the Most Fateful Decision of Your Life.* New York: Bobbs-Merrill, 1980.

Wilt, Joy. *Happily Ever After.* Waco, Tex.: Word, 1977.*

_____. *An Uncomplicated Guide to Becoming a Superparent.* Waco, Tex.: Word, 1977.*

## Single Parenting

Atkin, Edith, and Rubin, Estelle. *Part-Time Father: A Guide for the Divorced Father.* New York: Vanguard, 1976.

Carter, Velma, and Leavenworth, J. Lynn. *Putting the Pieces Together: Help for Single Parents.* Valley Forge, Penn.: Judson Press, 1977.

Gatley, Richard H., and Koulack, David. *Single Father's Handbook: A Guide for Separated and Divorced Fathers.* Garden City, N.Y.: Anchor Press/Doubleday, 1979.*

Klein, Carole. *The Single Parent Experience.* New York: Avon, 1973.*

Rowlands, Peter. *Saturday Parent: A Book for Separated Families.* New York: Continuum, 1980.

# Family Enrichment

Agard, Bonnie. *Family Cluster Resources*. Chicago: Department of Christian Education, The Evangelical Covenant Church, 1977. (Basics for family cluster education; activities for 17 sessions provided.)

Carnes, Patrick. *Understanding Us: A Family Development Experience*. Minneapolis: Interpersonal Communication Program, Inc., 1981. (An excellent intergenerational program based on Olson's "circumplex" model of family functioning.)

*Family Enrichment Workshop*. Board of Christian Education, Church of God, P.O. Box 2458, Anderson, Ind., 46018. (Leader's Guide and Participants' Resources are available.)

*The Family Weekend Experience*. New York: William H. Sadlier, 1976. (Excellent kit of creative activities for a family enrichment weekend. Includes guide, visuals, cassettes, filmstrips.)

Gallagher, Maureen. *Op. Family*. Paramus, N.J.: Paulist Press.*

Haessly, Jacqueline. *Peacemaking: Family Activities for Peace and Justice*. New York: Paulist Press, 1981.*

Kelmer, Richard H., and Smith, Rebecca M. *Teaching About Family Relationships*. Minneapolis: Burgess, 1975.*

Koehler, George E. *Learning Together: A Guide for Intergenerational Education in the Church*. Nashville: Discipleship Resources, 1977.*

Leonard, Joe. *Church Family Gatherings: Programs and Plans*. Valley Forge, Pa.: Judson Press, 1978.

Logan, Ben, and Moody, Kate, eds. *Television Awareness Training: The Viewer's Guide for Family and Community*. Nashville: Abingdon, 1980.

Nutting, R. Ted. *Family Cluster Programs*. Valley Forge, Pa.: Judson Press, 1978.

Otto, Herbert. *The Use of Family Strength Concepts and Methods in Family Life Education*. Beverly Hills, Calif.: The Holistic Press, 1975.*

*Paths of Life: Family Life Programs*. New York: Paulist Press, 1980.

Purnell, D. *Working with Families*. Rochester, N.Y.: Family Clustering, 1980.*

Rogers, Jack, and Rogers, Sharee. *The Family Together: Inter-Generational Education in the Church School*. Los Angeles: Action House, 1976.*

Rugh, Jan. "Suggested Resource List for Family Clusters." Rochester, N.Y.: Family Clustering, 1975. (Includes songs, audiovisuals, etc.)

Sawin, Margaret M. "Educating by Family Groups: A New Model for Religious Education." Rochester, N.Y.: Family Clustering, 1977.

_____ . *Family Enrichment with Family Clusters*. Valley Forge, Pa.: Judson Press, 1979.

_____ . *Hope for Families*. New York: Sadlier, 1982.

_____ . "Purple Tree" Newsletter. Rochester, N.Y.: Family Clustering.

_____ . "Resources for Further Research in Family Education." Rochester, N.Y.: Family Clustering, 1982.

*Together: A Guide for Leaders of Intergenerational Events*. Philadelphia: Fortress Press, 1984.

Williams, Mel, and Brittain, Mary Ann. *Christian Education in Family Clusters*. Valley Forge, Pa.: Judson Press, 1982.

## Resources for Families

Baratta-Lorton, Mary. *Workjobs for Parents: Activity Centered Learning in the Home*. Menlo Park, Calif.: Addison-Wesley, 1975.*

Bock, Lois, and Working, Miji. *Happiness Is a Family Time Together*. Old Tappan, N.J.: Fleming H. Revell, 1977.*

Brayer, Herbert, and Brayer, Zella. *Valuing in the Family*. San Diego, Calif.: Pennant Press, 1972.*

Brusius, Ron, and Noettl, Margaret. *Family Evening Activity Devotions*. St. Louis: Concordia, 1980.

Fiarotta, Phillis, and Fiarotta, Noel. *Be What You Want to Be!* New York: Workman, 1977.

_____ . *The You and Me Heritage Tree*. New York: Workman, 1976.*

Jenkins, Jeanne, and MacDonald, Pam. *Growing Up Equal*. Englewood Cliffs, N.J.: Prentice-Hall, 1979.*

Kubler-Ross, Elisabeth. *To Live Until We Say Good-bye*. Englewood Cliffs, N.J.: Prentice-Hall, 1978.

Rickerson, Wayne. *Good Times for Your Family*. Ventura, Calif.: Regal Books, 1977.*

Rogers, Fred. *Many Ways to Say I Love You*. Valley Forge, Pa.: Judson, 1977.

Shedd, Charlie. *Grandparents: Then God Created Grandparents and It Was Very Good*. Garden City, N.Y.: Doubleday, 1976.

Shephard, Mary, and Shephard, Ray. *Vegetable Soup Activities*. New York: Citation Press, 1975. Multicultural family experiences.*

Sloane, Valerie. *Creative Family Activities*. Nashville: Abingdon, 1976.*

Wilt, Joy, and Watson, Terre. *Seasonal and Holiday Happenings.* Waco, Tex.: Word, 1978. (One of a number of resources in the Can-Make-and-Do series.)*

# Family Counseling

## Marriage and Family Counseling

Atkinson, Donald R., and Morten, George. *Counseling American Minorities: A Cross-Cultural Perspective.* 2nd ed. Dubuque, Iowa: Wm. C. Brown Company, 1982.

Bandler, Richard; Grinder, John; and Satir, Virginia. *Changing with Families: A Book About Further Education for Being Human.* Palo Alto, Calif.: Science and Behavior Books, 1976. (Excellent resources on family therapy.)*

Corey, Gerald. *Theory and Practice of Counseling and Psychotherapy.* 3rd ed. Monterey, Calif.: Brooks/Cole Publishing Company, 1985. (An excellent training program. A manual is also available.)

Glick, Ira D., and Kessler, David R, eds. *Marital and Family Therapy: An Introductory Text.* 2nd ed. New York: Grune & Stratton, 1980.

Hatton, Corrine Lois; Valente, Sharon McBride; and Rink, Alice. *Suicide: Assessment and Intervention.* 2nd ed. New York: Appleton-Century-Crofts, 1983.

Jones, Hardin B., and Jones, Helen C. *Sensual Drugs: Deprivation and Rehabilitation of the Mind.* New York: Cambridge University Press, 1977.

Lieb, Julian; Raymond, Margaret; and Slaby, Andrew. *The Healing Alliance: A New View of the Family's Role in the Treatment of Emotional Problems.* New York: W. W. Norton & Company, Inc., 1975.*

Looff, David H. *Getting to Know the Troubled Child.* Knoxville, Tenn.: University of Tennessee Press, 1976. (Helpful guidelines for the evaluation of troubled children and their situations. Helps for family therapy as well.)*

Luthman, Shirley, and Kirschenbaum, Martin. *The Dynamic Family.* Palo Alto, Calif.: Science and Behavior Books, Inc., 1974. (Excellent foundation for family therapy.)

Minuchin, Salvador. *Families and Family Therapy.* Cambridge, Mass.: Harvard University Press, 1974.

Moustakas, Clark. *Who Will Listen? Children and Parents in Therapy.* New York: Ballantine Books, 1975. (Helpful guidelines for listening, being honest and compassionate, especially for the therapeutic setting.)*

Neuhaus, Robert, and Neuhaus, Ruby. *Family Crises.* Columbus, Ohio: Charles E. Merrill Publishing Company, 1974. (Deals with retardation, crime and delinquency, unplanned pregnancy, drug abuse, alcoholism, divorce, mental illness, mid-life and later-life adjustments.)*

Pelletier, Kenneth R. *Mind as Healer, Mind as Slayer: A Holistic Approach to Preventing Stress Disorders.* Magnolia, Mass.: Peter Smith Publisher Inc., 1984.

Satir, Virginia. *Conjoint Family Therapy.* 3rd ed. Palo Alto, Calif.: Science and Behavior Books, Inc., 1983.

Stierlin, Helm; Rucker-Embden, Ingebord; Wetzel, Norbert; and Wirsching, Michael. *The First Interview with the Family.* New York: Brunner/Mazel, 1980.

Stuart, Richard B. *Helping Couples Change: A Social Learning Approach to Marital Therapy.* New York: The Guilford Press, 1980.

Walrond-Skinner, Sue. *Family Therapy: The Treatment of Natural Systems.* Boston: Routledge & Kegan Paul, 1977.

## Pastoral Counseling

Anderson, Douglas, A. *New Approaches to Family Pastoral Care.* Philadelphia: Fortress Press, 1980.

Augsburger, David W. *Anger and Assertiveness in Pastoral Care.* Philadelphia: Fortress Press, 1979.

Clinebell, Howard J. *Growth Counseling.* Nashville: Abingdon, 1979.

_____ . *Growth Counseling for Marriage Enrichment: Pre-Marriage and the Early Years.* Philadelphia: Fortress Press, 1975.

Colston, Lowell G. *Pastoral Care with Handicapped Persons.* Philadelphia: Fortress Press, 1978.

Costales, Clarie, and Berry, Jo. *Alcoholism: The Way Back to Reality.* Ventura, Calif.: Regal Books, 1980.*

Mace, David, and Mace, Vera. *What's Happening to Clergy Marriages?* Nashville: Abingdon, 1980.

Oates, Wayne E. *Pastoral Care and Counseling in Grief and Separation.* Philadelphia: Fortress Press, 1976.

Ogden, Thomas C. *Guilt Free.* Nashville: Abingdon, 1980.*

Oglesby, William B., Jr. *Biblical Themes for Pastoral Counseling.* Nashville: Abingdon, 1978.

Stewart, Charles William. *The Minister as Family Counselor.* Nashville: Abingdon, 1978.*

Stone, Howard W. *Crisis Counseling.* Philadelphia: Fortress Press, 1976.

Welter, Paul. *Family Problems and Predicaments: How to Respond.* Wheaton, Ill.: Tyndale House Publishers Inc., 1977. (Christian resources for dealing with family crises.)*

Wilke, Harold H. *Creating the Caring Congregation: Guidelines for Ministering with the Handicapped.* Nashville: Abingdon, 1980.

Wilke, Richard B. *The Pastor and Marriage Group Counseling.* Nashville: Abingdon, 1974.*

Wimberley, Edward P. *Pastoral Care in the Black Church.* Nashville: Abingdon, 1979.

————— . "Pastoral Counseling and the Black Perspective." *Journal of Pastoral Care* 30 (December 1976).

## Training Organizations

The following list provides the names and addresses of several organizations which offer leadership training opportunities for persons desiring enhancement of their skills in leading marriage and family enrichment events. There are also many church and community groups which may offer such training, as well as enrichment events for couples and families.

AMERICAN ASSOCIATION FOR MARRIAGE AND FAMILY THERAPY
1717 K Street, NW. Suite 407
Washington DC 20006

AMERICAN ASSOCIATION FOR SEX EDUCATORS, COUNSELORS, AND THERAPISTS
5010 Wisconsin Avenue, NW Suite 304
Washington DC 20006

ASSOCIATION OF COUPLES FOR MARRIAGE ENRICHMENT
459 S. Church Street    PO Box 10596
Winston-Salem NC 27108

FAMILY CLUSTERING, INC.
124 Clinton Street
Tonawanda NY 14150

FAMILY SERVICE AMERICA
   44 E. 23rd Street
   New York NY 10010

INTERPERSONAL COMMUNICATION PROGRAMS
   1925 Nicollet Avenue
   Minneapolis MN 55403

NATIONAL COUNCIL OF CHURCHES
   Commission on Family Ministries and Human Sexuality
   475 Riverside Drive Room 708
   New York NY 10115-0050

NATIONAL COUNCIL ON FAMILY RELATIONS
   1910 W. County Road B. Suite 147
   St. Paul MN 55113

NATIONAL INSTITUTE FOR THE FAMILY
   3019 4th St., NE
   Washington DC 20017

NATIONAL PARENTING FOR PEACE AND JUSTICE NETWORK
   4144 Lindell Blvd. Suite 400
   St. Louis MO 63108

# PART FIVE
# Reproduction Masters

# The Family Life Cycle                                              RM 1

*Note:* While these stages do occur in many families, they are by no means universal. For example, a couple may not have any children. Or a divorce may occur. And such people may or may not get remarried. In one sense, every family will have its own "ages and stages," depending upon what happens within the family itself.

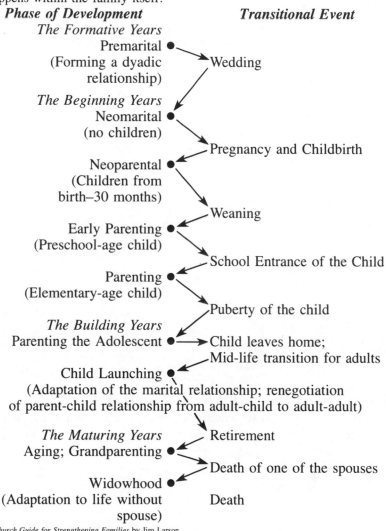

*Phase of Development*         *Transitional Event*

    *The Formative Years*

Premarital ●       Wedding
(Forming a dyadic
relationship)

*The Beginning Years*
Neomarital ●
(no children)

      Pregnancy and Childbirth

Neoparental ●
(Children from
birth–30 months)

      Weaning

Early Parenting ●
(Preschool-age child)

      School Entrance of the Child

Parenting ●
(Elementary-age child)

      Puberty of the child

*The Building Years*
Parenting the Adolescent ● ⟶ Child leaves home;
      Mid-life transition for adults

Child Launching ●
(Adaptation of the marital relationship; renegotiation
of parent-child relationship from adult-child to adult-adult)

*The Maturing Years*   Retirement
Aging; Grandparenting ●

      Death of one of the spouses

Widowhood ●
(Adaptation to life without   Death
spouse)

# Family Ministry through the Life Cycle

**RM 2**

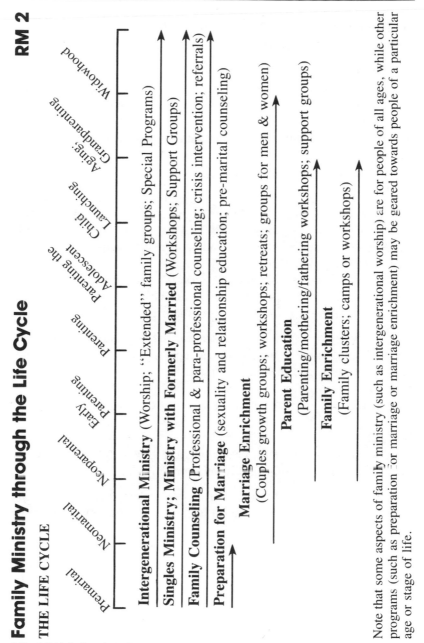

## THE LIFE CYCLE

Premarital · Neonatal · Neoparental · Early Parenting · Parenting · Parenting the Adolescent · Child Launching · Aging; Grandparenting · Widowhood

**Intergenerational Ministry** (Worship; "Extended" family groups; Special Programs)

**Singles Ministry; Ministry with Formerly Married** (Workshops; Support Groups)

**Family Counseling** (Professional & para-professional counseling; crisis intervention; referrals)

**Preparation for Marriage** (sexuality and relationship education; pre-marital counseling)

    **Marriage Enrichment**
      (Couples growth groups; workshops; retreats; groups for men & women)

        **Parent Education**
          (Parenting/mothering/fathering workshops; support groups)

          **Family Enrichment**
            (Family clusters; camps or workshops)

Note that some aspects of family ministry (such as intergenerational worship) are for people of all ages, while other programs (such as preparation for marriage or marriage enrichment) may be geared towards people of a particular age or stage of life.

# Evaluation Tool for Developing Family Awareness

RM 3

## Calendar

A. Review the calendar found in your church bulletin for a typical month. List the times and descriptions of various events for each day. Identify the intended audience (e.g., men, women, children, etc.) for each program. (You may want to map this out on a large sheet of butcher paper.)

| Sunday | Monday | Tuesday | Wednesday | Thursday | Friday | Saturday |
|--------|--------|---------|-----------|----------|--------|----------|
|        |        |         |           |          |        |          |

B. Evaluate the impact of the church's schedule on families. (You may want to take a typical family or two—such as a family with young children, and a family with adolescent children—and describe their involvement in church life.)

- Does the church calendar encourage quality time for families?
- Does the church sponsor specific activities which involve family members together and strengthen family relationships?

C. Review your church's calendar for the previous year (such as may be found in the church's annual report). List specific activities designed to enhance marriage relationships, parenting skills, or to provide intergenerational enrichment (two or more generations meeting together for an educational or worship event).

## Budget

A. Review the previous year's budget. List specific allocations and their intended use in family ministry.

B. Evaluate your church's priorities as reflected in the calendar and budget—especially in relation to the needs of couples, parents, and families.

# Qualities of a Healthy Marriage and Family

**RM 4**

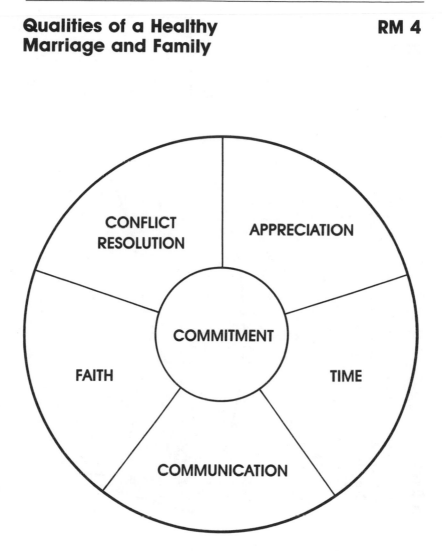

**RM 5**

# Bridge Building Exercise

1. Identify ways in which each person is unique/different. List these items under each name.
2. Identify ways (similar interests, beliefs, likes, dislikes, etc.) in which the two of you are similar. List these items on the "bridge" between the two names.

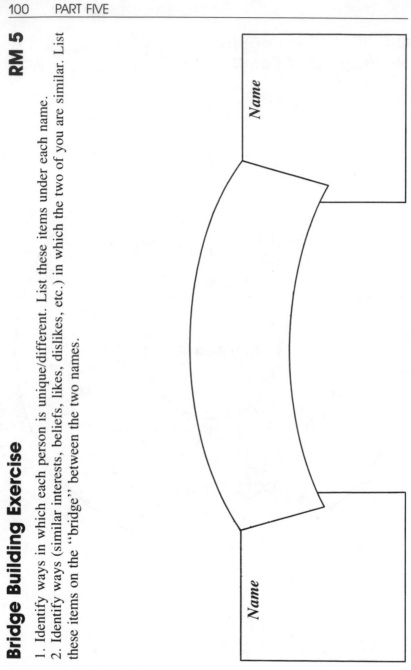

*Name*

*Name*

# Marriage Time Line

**RM 6**

**1.** List several major changes or crises (either positive or negative) that have happened to you or your family since you have been married.

1. _____
2. _____
3. _____
4. _____
5. _____
6. _____
7. _____
8. _____
9. _____

**2.** Now plot these events on the time line below. Place the event above the line if it was primarily positive when it occurred, below the line if it was primarily negative, and on the line if it was neutral (see sample time line).

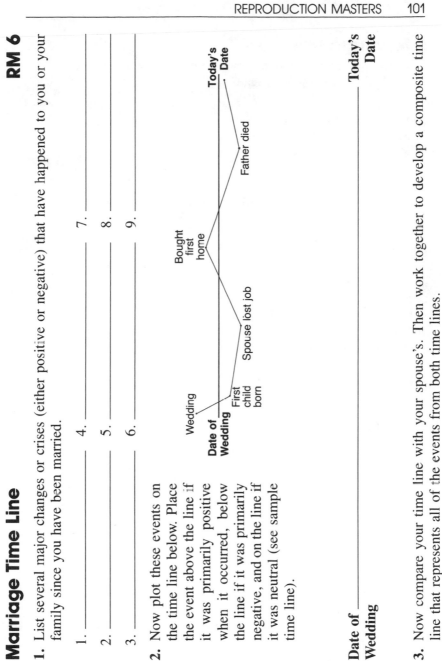

**Date of Wedding** — Wedding — First child born — Spouse lost job — Bought first home — Father died — **Today's Date**

**Date of Wedding** _____ **Today's Date**

**3.** Now compare your time line with your spouse's. Then work together to develop a composite time line that represents all of the events from both time lines.

# A Marriage Inventory                                        RM 7

**1.** Circle a number which indicates your response to each statement as it relates to your marriage.

| | NOT YET BEGUN | MOSTLY UNSATISFACTORY | | ACCEPTABLE | VERY SATISFACTORY |
|---|---|---|---|---|---|
| A. We are "unhooked" from our parents; they treat us as adults. | 0 | 1 | 2 | 3   4 | 5 |
| B. As a couple, we have a lot of fun together. | 0 | 1 | 2 | 3   4 | 5 |
| C. We share many of the same values. | 0 | 1 | 2 | 3   4 | 5 |
| D. We share the same religious beliefs. | 0 | 1 | 2 | 3   4 | 5 |
| E. We have worked to develop healthy communication skills. | 0 | 1 | 2 | 3   4 | 5 |
| F. We cope with crisis and stress constructively. | 0 | 1 | 2 | 3   4 | 5 |
| G. We have a satisfying sex life. | 0 | 1 | 2 | 3   4 | 5 |
| H. Our needs for affection are met. | 0 | 1 | 2 | 3   4 | 5 |
| I. We regularly express appreciation to each other. | 0 | 1 | 2 | 3   4 | 5 |
| J. We encourage each other to grow personally. | 0 | 1 | 2 | 3   4 | 5 |
| K. We each have outside interests. | 0 | 1 | 2 | 3   4 | 5 |
| L. We maintain a healthy balance between our marriage relationship and other aspects of our lives (jobs, children, etc.) | 0 | 1 | 2 | 3   4 | 5 |

**2.** Now total the score of the numbers you have circled. Where are you on a scale of 0 to 60? _____ .

**3.** Now compare your responses with your spouse's and discuss any differences.

## Resources for Couples   (Side 1)    RM 8

Here is a basic list of resources which can help strengthen your relationship as a couple, as well as enhance your personal growth.

### Sexuality/Sex Roles

Barbach, Lonnie. *For Yourself: The Fulfillment of Female Sexuality.* Garden City, N.Y.: Anchor Press/Doubleday, 1976.

Dowling, Colette. *The Cinderella Complex: Women's Hidden Fear of Independence.* New York: Summit Books, 1982.

Friday, Nancy. *My Mother, My Self.* New York: Dell Publishing Co., 1981.

Jewett, Paul K. *Man as Male and Female.* Grand Rapids, Mich.: Eerdmans, 1975.

Lipman-Blumen, Jean. *Gender Roles and Power.* Englewood Cliffs, N.J.: Prentice-Hall, 1984.

Nelson, James. *Embodiment.* Minneapolis: Augsburg, 1979.

Olson, Richard. *Changing Male Roles in Today's World: A Christian Perspective for Men—and the Women Who Care about Them.* Valley Forge, Pa.: Judson, 1982.

Penner, Clifford, and Penner, Joyce. *The Gift of Sex.* Waco, Tex.: Word Books, 1981.

Sangiuliano, Iris. *In Her Time.* New York: Morrow Quill Paperbacks, 1980.

Smedes, Lewis B. *Sex for Christians.* Grand Rapids, Mich.: Eerdmans, 1976.

### Marriage

Augsburger, David. *Caring Enough to Confront.* Ventura, Calif.: Regal, 1980.

_____ . *When Enough Is Enough.* Ventura, Calif.: Regal, 1984.

Chartier, Jan, and Chartier, Myron. *Trusting Together in God.* St. Meinrad, Ind.: Abbey, 1984.

Demarest, Gary. *Christian Alternatives Within Marriage.* Waco, Tex.: Word, 1978.*

Halpern, Howard. *Cutting Loose: An Adult Guide to Coming to Terms with Your Parents.* New York: Bantam Books, 1978.

# Resources for Couples   (Side 2)        **RM 8**

Hunt, Joan, and Hunt, Richard. *Growing Love in Christian Marriage*. Nashville: The United Methodist Publishing House, 1981.

Mace, David R. *Success in Marriage*. Nashville: Abingdon, 1980.

Mace, David, and Mace, Vera. *How to Have a Happy Marriage*. Nashville: Abingdon, 1977.*

Miller, Sherod; Nunnally, Elam W.; and Wackman, Daniel B. *Couple Communication 1: Talking Together*. Minneapolis: Interpersonal Communication Programs, 1979.

Powell, John. *The Secret of Staying in Love*. Niles, Ill.: Argus, 1974.

Rubin, Lillian. *Intimate Strangers: Men and Women Together*. New York: Harper & Row, 1984.

Sheehy, Gail. *Pathfinders*. New York: Bantam, 1982.

Tournier, Paul. *To Understand Each Other*. Richmond, Va.: John Knox Press, 1967.

## Divorce and Remarriage

Adam, John, and Adam, Nancy. *Divorce: How and When to Let Go*. Englewood Cliffs, N.J.: Prentice-Hall, 1979.

Block, Joel. *To Marry Again*. New York: Grossett & Dunlap, 1979.*

Duncan, T. Roger, and Duncan, Darlene. *You're Divorced, But Your Children Aren't*. Englewood Cliffs, N.J.: Prentice-Hall, 1979.

Gardner, Richard A. *The Parent's Book About Divorce*. Garden City, N.Y.: Doubleday, 1979.

Levinger, George, and Motes, Oliver. *Divorce and Separation*. New York: Basic Books, 1979.

Small, Dwight H. *The Right to Remarry*. Old Tappan, N.J.: Revell, 1975.*

Smoke, Jim. *Growing Through Divorce*. Irvine, Calif.: Harvest House, 1976.

_____ . *Suddenly Single*. Old Tappan, N.J.: Revell, 1982.

Wallerstein, Judith S., and Kelly, Joan. *Surviving the Breakup: How Children and Parents Cope with Divorce*. New York: Basic Books, 1982.

Westoff, Leslie A. *The Second Time Around*. New York: Viking, 1977.*

*An asterisk (\*) indicates a book is out of print. In this case, the book may be found at a library or a resource center.*

# When I Stop to Think about It. . . .    RM 9

1. Circle a number which indicates your response to each of the qualities of health as it relates to your family.

|  | NOT YET BEGUN | MOSTLY UNSATISFACTORY | | ACCEPTABLE | VERY SATISFACTORY |
|---|---|---|---|---|---|
| A. Frequent expressions of appreciation to each other. | 0 | 1 | 2 | 3  4 | 5 |
| B. An adequate quantity and quality of time spent together (having fun, working together, etc.) | 0 | 1 | 2 | 3  4 | 5 |
| C. Healthy communication and listening skills. | 0 | 1 | 2 | 3  4 | 5 |
| D. High degree of commitment of family members to each other. | 0 | 1 | 2 | 3  4 | 5 |
| E. Common values and religious beliefs. | 0 | 1 | 2 | 3  4 | 5 |
| F. Effective crisis management skills. | 0 | 1 | 2 | 3  4 | 5 |

2. Now total the score of the numbers you have circled. Where are you on a scale from 0 to 30? _____ .

3. List these qualities of family health from most urgently needed in your family to least urgently needed.

- _____ most urgently needs attention
- _____
- _____
- _____
- _____
- _____ least urgently needs attention

RM 10

# Styles of Parenting

There are three basic styles of parenting: authoritarian, democratic, and permissive. As you think about each style, jot down words which describe them.

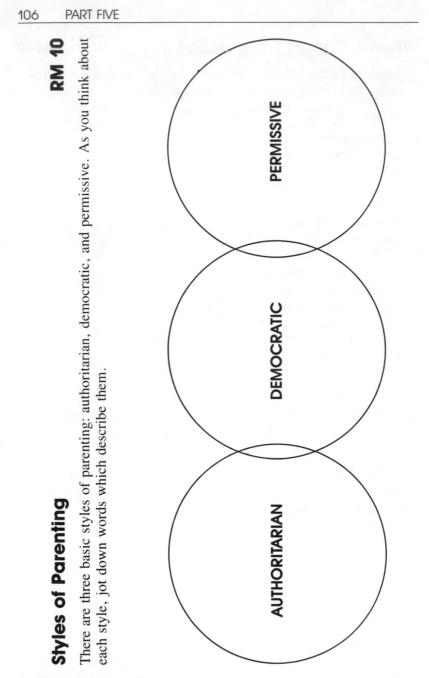

AUTHORITARIAN

DEMOCRATIC

PERMISSIVE

# Evaluating My Own Style of Parenting  RM 11

1. When I hear the word *authoritarian*, the following words come to mind:

_____    _____    _____

2. When I hear the word *permissive*, the following words come to mind:

_____    _____    _____

3. When I hear the word *democratic*, the following words come to mind:

_____    _____    _____

4. On the continuum below, place an *X* to mark where you think your general style of parenting is. Then place an *0* where you would like to be

_____

AUTHORITARIAN                    DEMOCRATIC                    PERMISSIVE

In order to make any change in parenting style, what steps will you need to take?

- _____
- _____
- _____

# Personally Speaking                              RM 12

As you stop for a moment and reflect on the kind of model or example you are to your children, what conclusions do you make about the following areas? (check one response for each area)

| | I WANT MY CHILDREN TO IMITATE ME | I DO NOT WANT MY CHILDREN TO IMITATE ME |
|---|---|---|
| 1. Your values | | |
| 2. Your religious beliefs | | |
| 3. The way you relate to others | | |
| 4. The way you handle feelings and conflicts | | |
| 5. Your attitude towards yourself (self-esteem) | | |
| 6. The way you handle money | | |
| 7. The way you handle time (balance of work, leisure, study, etc.) | | |
| 8. Other: _____ | | |
| 9. Other: _____ | | |

In order to be a more effective model to your children, identify one of these areas in which you would like to make a major change:

_____

The steps you will need to take to accomplish this goal are:

- _____
- _____
- _____
- _____

# Joys and Frustrations of Family Life     RM 13

Sometimes personal and family needs may be in conflict. In the left column, list personal needs you have (e.g., for love, companionship, job fulfillment, schooling, friends, "space," etc.). In the right column, list family needs you are aware of (e.g., finances, closeness, independence of children, responsibility, etc.). Then draw a line from any personal needs to any family needs which may represent a potential conflict.

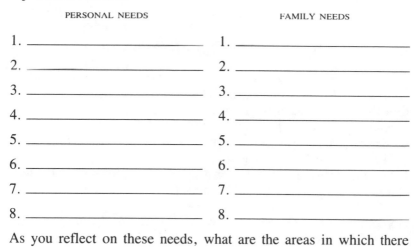

PERSONAL NEEDS                FAMILY NEEDS

1. _____     1. _____

2. _____     2. _____

3. _____     3. _____

4. _____     4. _____

5. _____     5. _____

6. _____     6. _____

7. _____     7. _____

8. _____     8. _____

As you reflect on these needs, what are the areas in which there may be the greatest conflict?_____ and _____.

To express your commitment to your family while remaining aware of your own personal needs, what steps will you take to resolve these conflicts?

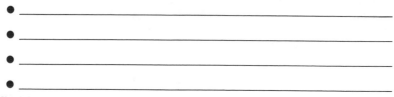

● _____

● _____

● _____

● _____

# Resources for Parents    (Side 1)    RM 14

Here is a basic list of resources which can strengthen your parenting skills.

## Parenting

Bell, Ruth, and Wildflower, Leni. *Talking with Your Teenagers: A Book for Parents.* New York: Random House, 1984.

Benson, Dennis C., and Stewart, Stan J. *The Ministry of the Child.* Nashville: Abingdon, 1979.

Bittman, Sam, and Zalk, Sue. *Expectant Fathers.* New York: Hawthorne, 1979.

Briggs, Dorothy C. *Your Child's Self-Esteem.* Garden City, N.Y.: Doubleday, 1970.

Buth, Lenore. *Sexuality: God's Precious Gift to Parents and Children.* St. Louis: Concordia, 1983.*

Calderone, Mary, and Johnson, Eric. *The Family Book About Sexuality.* New York: Harper and Row, 1981.

Calderone, Mary, and Ramey, James. *Talking with Your Child About Sex.* New York: Random House, 1982.

Fournier, Barbara, and Fournier, George. *Pre-Parenting: A Guide for Planning Ahead.* Englewood Cliffs, N.J.: Prentice-Hall, 1980.*

Gordon, Sol, and Gordon, Judith. *Raising a Child Conservatively in a Sexually Permissive World.* New York: Simon & Schuster, 1983.

Gordon, Thomas. *Parent Effectiveness Training.* New York: Wyden, 1970.

Johnson, Spencer. *The One Minute Father.* New York: William Morrow, 1983.

_____ . *The One Minute Mother.* New York: William Morrow, 1983.

Ketterman, Grace, and Ketterman, Herbert. *The Complete Book of Baby and Child Care for Christian Parents.* Old Tappan, N.J.: Fleming H. Revell, 1981.

Larson, Jim. *Growing a Healthy Family.* Minneapolis: Augsburg, 1986.

_____ . *Rights, Wrongs, and In-Betweens: Guiding Our Children to Christian Maturity.* Minneapolis: Augsburg, 1984.

# Resources for Parents  (Side 2)    RM 14

Lerman, Saf. *Parent Awareness*. Minneapolis: Winston, 1980.

Lewis, Jerry M. *How's Your Family?* New York: Brunner/Mazel, 1979.

McDermott, Joan. *Raising Cain (& Abel, Too): The Parent's Book of Sibling Rivalry*. New York: Wyden, 1980.*

McGinnis, Kathleen, and McGinnis, James. *Parenting for Peace and Justice*. Maryknoll, N.Y.: Orbis Books, 1981.

Miller, Mary Susan. *Child-Stress!* Garden City, N.Y.: Doubleday, 1982.*

Oates, Wayne, ed. Christian Care Books. Philadelphia: Westminster Press. (A wide variety of family issues.)

Oraker, James. *Almost Grown: A Christian Guide for Parents of Teenagers*. San Francisco: Harper and Row, 1980.

Rogers, Fred, and Head, Barry. *Mister Rogers Talks with Parents*. New York: Berkley Books, 1985.

Satir, Virginia. *Peoplemaking*. Palo Alto, Calif.: Science & Behavior Books, 1972.*

Scanzoni, Letha. *Sex Is a Parent Affair*. 2nd ed. New York: Bantam, 1982.*

Westerhoff, John H. *Bringing Up Children in the Christian Faith*. Minneapolis: Winston Press, 1980.

## Single Parenting

Atkin, Edith, and Rubin, Estell. *Part-Time Father*. New York: Vanguard, 1976.

Carter, Velma, and Leavenworth, J. Lynn. *Putting the Pieces Together*. Valley Forge, Pa.: Judson, 1977.

Rowlands, Peter. *Saturday Parent: A Book for Separated Families*. New York: Continuum, 1982.

## Stepparenting

Berman, Claire. *Making It as a Stepparent*. Garden City, N.Y.: Doubleday, 1980.*

Kalter, Suzy. *Instant Parent*. New York: A and W Publishers, 1979.*

Reed, Bobbie. *Stepfamilies*. St. Louis, Mo.: Concordia, 1980.*

Visher, Emily, and Visher, John. *Stepfamilies: A Guide to Working with Stepparents and Stepchildren*. New York: Brunner/Mazel, 1980.

*An asterisk (\*) indicates a book is out of print. In this case, the book may be found at a library or resource center.*

# Wacky Words 1                                    RM 15

The object of these brain teasers is to discern a familiar word, phrase, saying, or name from each arrangement of letters and/or symbols. For example, box 1a below depicts "two eggs over easy." Box 1b shows "cornerstone." Write your answer in each box.

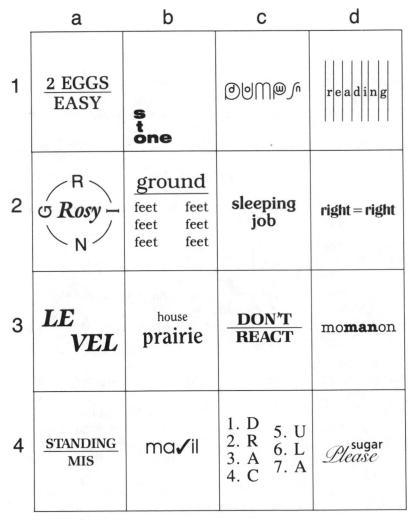

|   | a | b | c | d |
|---|---|---|---|---|
| 1 | 2 EGGS EASY | s t one | ⓓⓤⓜⓟⓢ | reading |
| 2 | R ↺ Rosy N | ground / feet feet / feet feet / feet feet | sleeping job | right = right |
| 3 | LE VEL | house prairie | DON'T REACT | momanon |
| 4 | STANDING MIS | ma✓il | 1. D  2. R  3. A  4. C  5. U  6. L  7. A | Please sugar |

# Family Fun Songs                                    RM 16

### My Bonnie Lies Over the Ocean
My bonnie lies over the ocean, my bonnie lies over the sea;
My bonnie lies over the ocean, O bring back my bonnie to me.
Bring back, bring back, O bring back my bonnie to me, to me.
Bring back, bring back, O bring back my bonnie to me.

(*Note:* A fun way to sing this song is to stand up or sit down each time you come to a word beginning with the letter *B*. For example, the group stands up when singing the first "bonnie," then sits down again when singing the second "bonnie," and so on.)

### Row, Row, Row Your Boat (Traditional American Round)
Row, row, row your boat, gently down the stream.
Merrily, merrily, merrily, merrily, life is but a dream.

(*Note:* An interesting variation on this song is to sing it several times. The first time, you sing through the entire song. The second time, you sing through the whole song but leave off the word "dream." The next time, you leave off the words "a dream." And so on you go, leaving off one more word each time, until you end up with no words at all!)

### The Jay-Bird Song
Way down yonder not so very far off,
A jay-bird died of the whooping cough.
He whooped so hard with the whooping cough,
That he whooped his head and his tail right off.

(*Note:* This song is spoken rather than sung. The first verse begins with a whisper. At the end of the first verse, you say: "Same song, second verse, a little bit louder and a little bit worse." Each verse gets louder and louder, until the seventh verse, when everyone yells as loud as they can.)

### Mrs. Murphy's Chowder
Who put the blue jeans in Mrs. Murphy's chowder?
Nobody knows, so we'll ask a little louder.

(*Note:* As with the "Jay-Bird Song," this song is not sung but spoken. Each verse gets louder and louder.)

### A B C (for families with young children)
A-b-c-d-e-f-g; h-i-j-k-l-m-n-o-p.
Q-r-s-t-u-v; w-x-y and z;
Now I've sung my A-b-c's; next time won't you sing with me.

## What the World Needs Now. . . .    RM 17

"So, faith by it-self, if it has no works, is dead." James 2:17

"Be angry, but do not sin; do not let the sun go down on your anger." Ephesians 4:26

"We who are strong ought to bear with the failings of the weak, and not to please ourselves." Romans 15:1

"You shall love your neighbor as yourself." Matthew 22:39

*"Speaking the truth in love, we are to grow up in every way into him who is the head, into Christ, from whom the whole body, joined and knit together by every joint with which it is supplied, when each part is working properly, makes bodily growth and upbuilds itself in love." Ephesians 4:15-16*

"For this is the message which you have heard from the beginning, that we should love one another." 1 John 3:11

*"Love is patient and kind; love is not jealous or boastful; it is not arrogant or rude. Love does not insist on its own way; it is not irritable or resentful; it does not rejoice at wrong, but rejoices in the right." 1 Corinthians 13:4-6*

"Be kind to one another, tender-hearted, forgiving one anoth-er, as God in Christ for-gave you." Ephe-sians 4:32

# Wacky Words 2                                  RM 18

The object of these brain teasers is to discern a familiar word, phrase, saying, or name from each arrangement of letters and/or symbols. For example, box 1a below depicts "man overboard." Write your answers in each box.

## Family Togetherness                    RM 19

### Husbands and Wives

Going out for dinner
Playing tennis
Bowling
Going out for lunch
Going to a movie
Weekend away alone

Weekend at home alone
   (with kids away)
Concert, play, etc.
Reading a book together
Listening to favorite music
Doing a project together

### Family Activities

Bicycling
Hiking
Picnicking
Swimming
Going to the zoo
Miniature golf
Going out for dessert
Going to the beach
Library
Park
Museums
Airport
Animal farm
Mountains
Playing charades
Fixing a broken toy
Painting a room

Visiting someone who is
   sick: _____
Helping a neighbor or
   friend by _____
Visiting dad's or mom's place
   of employment
Family night at the YMCA
Fishing
Boating
Shopping
Camping
Taking the bus to _____
Taking the train to _____
Gardening
Reading a story
Playing a game

# A Family Contract                              **RM 20**

As a family, plan the following activities together. Fill in the boxes
that are appropriate to your family. Plan what will happen, and the
approximate dates when each activity will happen. Be creative and
plan activities which will not involve a great deal of money.

| WHO? | WHAT? | WHEN? |
|------|-------|-------|
| Husband and wife alone | _____ | _____ |
| Father with child _____ | _____ | _____ |
| Father with child _____ | _____ | _____ |
| Father with child _____ | _____ | _____ |
| Mother with child _____ | _____ | _____ |
| Mother with child _____ | _____ | _____ |
| Mother with child _____ | _____ | _____ |
| Activity for whole family | _____ | _____ |
| Activity for whole family | _____ | _____ |
| Activity for our family to do with another family | _____ | _____ |
| Children with each other | _____ | _____ |

*PLEDGE:* We the _____ family will try to the
best of our ability to do these activities by _____ :
Signed:

Father: _____ Child: _____

Mother: _____ Child: _____

Child: _____ Child: _____

# Wacky Words 3
### RM 21

The object of these brain teasers is to discern a familiar word, phrase, saying, or name from each arrangement of letters and/or symbols. Write your answer in each box.

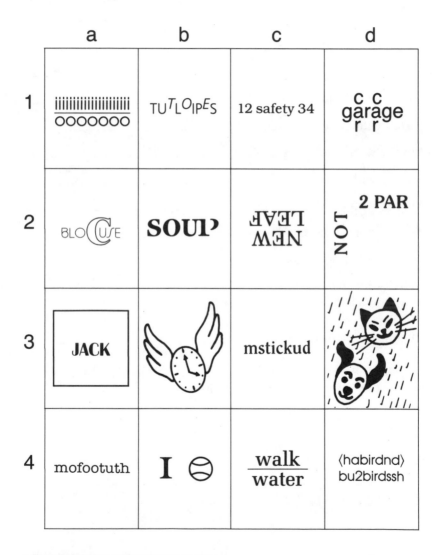

|   | a | b | c | d |
|---|---|---|---|---|
| 1 | iiiiiiiiiiiiiiiiiiiii OOOOOOO | TU ᵀLOₗₚEₛ | 12 safety 34 | c c garage r r |
| 2 | BLOᏟUᴤE | SOUᗡ | NEW LEAF (upside down) | NOT 2 PAR |
| 3 | JACK | (winged clock) | mstickud | (cat and dog in rain) |
| 4 | mofootuth | I ⊖ | walk / water | ⟨habirdnd⟩ bu2birdssh |

# Patterns of Communication                    RM 22

In her book *Peoplemaking,* Virginia Satir provides us with a helpful description of 5 basic communication patterns:

1. *Placater:* Such a person always agrees, trying to please. He or she is a person who often apologizes. The placater doesn't want anyone to be angry at him or her.

2. *Blamer:* Such a person is a fault-finder, dictator, boss. He or she acts superior, often to mask feelings of inferiority.

3. *Computer:* This communicator is ultra-reasonable, very correct. He or she does not show feelings, but appears to be calm, cool and collected. The computer carries many repressed feelings in his or her stomach.

4. *Distractor:* Such a person says and does what is irrelevant to what anyone else is saying or doing. He or she does not respond appropriately but often ignores others as they are talking and quickly changes the subject.

5. *Leveler:* Such a communicator is truthful, alive and free. The leveler's voice says words that match his facial expression, body position, and voice tone.

**Situation:** Your child wants to stay up past his or her bedtime to watch television. When you say, No, your child screams, "You're mean, mommy/daddy. You always treat me like a baby."

Let's think together of how people using each of these five communication patterns would respond to the child.

**Active Listening** (described by Thomas Gordon in *Parent Effectiveness Training):* is an effective way for a family to communicate. In using this method, parents are willing to take the time to listen to what children are saying and to understand what they are feeling. Parents do not initially feed back a message of their own, but what they feel the children's message meant. This empathetic listening process frees people to express their honest thoughts and feelings, knowing that they will not be quickly judged or "put down." The parent and child show respect for the honest communication of one for the other and try to clarify what is being communicated. "I" messages are used instead of "you" messages.

**Discussion:** Look back at the situation we have already discussed. Let's brainstorm together some responses to that child in which the parent utilizes active listening.

*A Church Guide for Strengthening Families* by Jim Larson

# Family Situations                          RM 23

Use the puppets your children have made. Act out each situation and complete the story. Switch roles by having the children play the part of the parents, and visa versa.

### Situation One:

Suzie/Johnny wants to buy a _____ because all of her/his friends have one. Her/his parents aren't too sure.

Suzie/Johnny: "I really want a _____ . All my friends have one. Why can't I have one, too? Don't you love me?"

### Situation Two:

Dad promises to take the family to the YMCA for a swim. But at the last minute, dad has to work late. The children are quite disappointed.

One child says, "Why do we always have to stay home? All my friends will be there. Dad sure is a spoil-sport!"

# Christian Songs for Families (Side 1)     RM 24

## Praise Him, Praise Him
*(A Song of Praise to Jesus)*

Praise Him, Praise Him,
Praise Him in the morning, Praise Him at the noontime.
Praise Him, Praise Him, Praise Him when the sun goes down.

*Additional verses:*
  Love Him. Serve Him. Thank Him.

## Come and Praise the Lord
*(Tune: "Michael Row the Boat Ashore")*

Come and praise the Lord our King, Alleluia.
Lift your voice and let us sing, Alleluia.
Christ was born in Bethlehem, Alleluia.
Son of God and Son of man, Alleluia.
He grew up an earthly child, Alleluia.
Of the world, but undefiled, Alleluia.
Jesus died at Calvary, Alleluia.
Rose again triumphantly, Alleluia.
He will cleanse us from our sin, Alleluia.
If we live by faith in him, Alleluia.
We will live with God some day, Alleluia.
And forever with God stay, Alleluia.

## God Is So Good

God is so good, God is so good,
God is so good, God's so good to me.

*Additional verses:*
  God is my friend. . . .
  God answers prayer . . .
  God loves me so . . .

# Christian Songs for Families (Side 2)    RM 24

### Kum Ba Yah
*(Translation: "Come by here, O Lord")*

Kum ba yah, my Lord, Kum ba yah! *(Repeat 3 times)*
Oh, Lord, Kum ba yah!

*Additional verses:*
Someone's crying, Lord, Kum ba yah!
Someone's praying, Lord, Kum ba yah!
Someone's singing, Lord, Kum ba yah!

### The Lord's Prayer
Our Father in heaven
hallowed be your name,
your kingdom come,
your will be done,
on earth as it is in heaven.
Give us today our daily bread.
Forgive us our sins
as we forgive those
who sin against us.
Save us from the time of trial
and deliver us from evil.
For the kingdom, the power,
and the glory are yours,
now and forever. Amen

# Brain Teasers (Side 1)                    RM 25

1. Write the year of your birth. Double it. Add 5. Multiply by 50. Add your age. Add 365. Subtract 615. What do you get?

2. A boy, driving some cows, was asked how many cows he had. He said, "When they are in line there are two cows ahead of a cow, two cows behind a cow, and one cow in the middle." How many cows did he have?

3. The hands of a clock indicate that the time is 1:20. If the hour hand were where the minute hand is and visa versa, what time (to the nearest five minutes) would it be?

4. If a pilot and copilot for a space flight are to be chosen from a group of five persons of different ages, and the older person must always be the pilot, how many different crews can be made up?

5. A frog at the bottom of a 40-foot well jumps up three feet every day and falls back two feet at night. How many days will it take him to get out of the well?

## Brain Teasers (Side 2)                    RM 25

6. If somebody bought something for $20, sold it for $30, repurchased it for $40, resold it for $50, how many dollars did he make?

7. When a boy opens his Christmas savings bank, he finds that he has just 100 coins in half dollars, dimes, and pennies. When he counts the money he finds that he has exactly $5.00. How many coins does he have of each denomination?

8. A man and woman agree to meet at three o'clock. However, unknown to the other, the man's watch is five minutes slow and the woman's watch is five minutes fast. If the man arrives for the appointment five minutes late by his watch and the woman is five minutes early by her watch, how many minutes will one person have to wait for the other?

9. A woman resolves to save a penny on January 1, two cents on January 2, and so on, doubling the amount saved on the previous day for the 31 days of January. How much would be saved in this way? Make a guess.

10. How much is 40 divided by ¼ plus 7?

# Writing a Cinquain Poem                    RM 26

We have been talking about how we can grow together as families.
Let's write a cinquain poem about some aspect of family life.
Start with one word (such as family, the Jones's, etc.). Then, all
the other words tell about the first word.

*Line 1:* Theme word (such as family).

*Line 2:* Two words that describe the theme word.

*Line 3:* Three words to describe some action related to the theme
word (often words ending in *ing* are used).

*Line 4:* Four words that describe your feelings about the theme
word.

*Line 5:* Another name (or synonym) for the theme word (or, use
the theme word again).

Use the blank lines below for your poem.

_____

_____   _____

_____   _____   _____

_____   _____   _____   _____

_____

## Resources for Families                          RM 27

Here is a list of books which describe a wide variety of activities for your family to enjoy together.

Baratta-Lorton, Mary. *Workjobs for Parents: Activity-Centered Learning in the Home.* Menlo Park, Calif.: Addison-Wesley, 1975.*

Bock, Lois, and Working, Miji. *Happiness Is a Family Time Together.* Old Tappan, N.J.: Fleming H. Revell, 1975.*

_____ . *Happiness Is a Family Walk with God.* Old Tappan, N.J.: Fleming H. Revell, 1977.*

Brayer, Herbert, and Brayer, Zella. *Valuing in the Family.* San Diego, Calif.: Pennant Press, 1972.*

Brusius, Ron, and Noettl, Margaret. *Family Evening Activity Devotions.* St. Louis, Mo.: Concordia, 1980.

Fiarotta, Phyllis, and Fiarotta, Noel. *Be What You Want to Be!* New York: Workman, 1977.

_____ . *The You and Me Heritage Tree.* New York: Workman, 1976.*

Jenkins, Jeanne, and MacDonald, Pam. *Growing Up Equal.* Englewood Cliffs, N.J.: Prentice-Hall, 1979.*

Kubler-Ross, Elisabeth. *To Live Until We Say Good-Bye.* Englewood Cliffs, N.J.: Prentice-Hall, 1978.

Rickerson, Wayne. *Good Times for Your Family.* Ventura, Calif.: Regal Books, 1977.*

Rogers, Fred. *Many Ways to Say I Love You.* Valley Forge, Pa.: Judson Press, 1977.

Shedd, Charlie. *Grandparents: Then God Created Grandparents and It Was Very Good.* Garden City, N.Y.: Doubleday, 1976.

Shephard, Mary, and Shephard, Ray. *Vegetable Soup Activities.* New York: Citation Press, 1975. (Multi-cultural family experiences.)*

Sloane, Valerie. *Creative Family Activities.* Nashville: Abingdon, 1976.*

Wilt, Joy, and Watson, Terre. *Seasonal and Holiday Happenings.* Waco, Tex.: Word, 1978.*

*An asterisk (\*) indicates a book is out of print. In this case, the book may be found in a library or a resource center.*

# Notes

## Part One

1. Albert J. Solnit, "Changing Psychological Perspectives About Children and Their Families," *Children Today,* May-June 1976, p. 9.
2. Gail Godwin, *A Mother and Two Daughters* (New York: Avon, 1982), p. 466.
3. Kenneth Keniston, *All Our Children* (New York: Harcourt, Brace, Jovanovich, 1977), p. 17.
4. Alvin Toffler, *Future Shock* (New York: Random House, 1970).
5. *Teenage Pregnancy: The Problem that Hasn't Gone Away* (New York: The Allan Guttmacher Institute, 1981), p. 7.
6. Ibid.
7. Gail Sheehy, *Pathfinders* (New York: Bantam Books, 1981).
8. Nick Stinnett, et. al., *Building Family Strengths: Blueprints for Action* (Lincoln, Nebraska: University of Nebraska Press, 1979).
9. Nick Stinnett, et. al., *Family Strengths: Positive Models for Family Life* (Lincoln, Nebraska: University of Nebraska Press, 1980), p. 2.
10. Dolores Curran, *Traits of a Healthy Family* (Minneapolis: Winston Press, 1983).

## Part Two

1. David Mace and Vera Mace, *Marriage Enrichment in the Church* (Nashville: Broadman, 1976), p. 34.
2. Virginia Satir, *Peoplemaking* (Palo Alto, California: Science and Behavior Books, 1972), p. 197.